My FAVORITE Story

Pathway
PRESS & RESOURCES

My FAVORITE Story

WALKING WITH JESUS III

TOBY S. MORGAN

Director of Publications: David H. Gosnell

Managing Editor of Publications: Lance Colkmire

Associate Editor: Arleah Waycaster

Editorial Assistant: Tammy Hatfield

Cover and Layout Design: Stephanie Grable

ISBN: 978-1-64288-387-9

Please direct inquiries to Pathway Press, 1080 Montgomery Avenue, Cleveland, TN 37311. *www.pathwaypress.org*

CONTENTS

FOREWORD 7

INTRODUCTION 9

The Greatest Sermon Ever

Part I 11

Part II 35

Part III 61

Part IV 85

A Good Roman 99

Who Does He Think He Is? 113

John: A Wondering Mystery 129

A Tale of Two Responses 141

He Said, She Said 155

A Day of Confrontation 169

Kingdom Stories 193

When a Long Day Ends with a Storm 211

My Favorite Story 227

FOREWORD

Perhaps like you, I am gripped with an all-consuming desire to know Jesus Christ—to be with Him, to follow Him, to be found in Him and conformed to His image, to even suffer with Him and, in so doing, experience the power that raised Him from the dead. Although I have walked with the Lord for much of my life, I keep getting this feeling that there is more. This quest has led me to read again every detail of the life and ministry of Jesus Christ.

Born contrary to every law of life, Jesus came to this earth and spoke with authority. His word was powerful, for "in Him all the fulness of Deity dwells in bodily form" (Colossians 2:9 NASB). He healed the brokenhearted, proclaimed freedom to those taken captive by Satan to do his will, healed multitudes of various diseases, and even raised the dead. Through His death, Jesus conquered the one who had the power of death and opened a new and living way for every human being to be ushered into the presence of God. No wonder people were amazed by Him!

Wherever Jesus went, multitudes gathered. Some pressed through crowds to get close enough to touch Him. Others climbed trees to catch a glimpse of Him. The blind cried out for Him. Even those tormented by demons fell at His feet and proclaimed Him to be the Son of God.

Jesus comforted the afflicted, afflicted the comfortable, and invited all to find rest in Him.

In *My Favorite Story*, Toby Morgan takes us on an unforgettable journey to see and experience this Jesus. An inimitable writer, he takes us from "now" to "then," from "here" to "there," and helps us to sense how it felt to be in Jesus' presence. It is almost like we are personally present listening to Jesus preach his famous "Sermon on the Mount," or outside the city of Nain watching Jesus encounter a grieving widow, or on that boat tossed by a storm, or at Gadara when a man from the tombs accosts Jesus. However, more than simply telling the stories, Bishop Morgan draws from them eternal truths that speak to our day, to our grief, to our storms.

I commend this marvelous book and the "Walking With the Master" series to you with full assurance that you will be blessed, strengthened, and edified. As you read, may "the God of our Lord Jesus Christ, the glorious Father, give you the Spirit of wisdom and revelation, so that you may know him better" (Ephesians 1:17 NIV).

Mark L. Williams, DMin.
Assistant General Overseer
Church of God

INTRODUCTION

My Favorite Story picks up the life of the Master sometime in the spring of His second year of ministry. Some date this compressed section of His life to 27 AD, but the exactness of the date is disputable. What matters to the believer is the amazing teaching and extraordinary power He displayed during this brief section of His life.

In this journey we will encounter and explore what we call the "Sermon on the Mount." I well remember Dr. Don Bowdle, famous for his instruction in systematic theology at Lee University, stressing to us in class one day the importance of this sermon. He said if we would take this sermon seriously and implement it into our lives, the church world would be radically changed overnight. I cannot dispute his belief.

As the tension brought to bear by the religious and governmental leadership was ratcheted up, Jesus moved from place to place, demonstrating the power of the Kingdom everywhere He went. By the time you reach the end of this volume, you will encounter Him in the middle of Gentile territory and discover His power is not limited to the confines of the church of His day. I call this volume *My Favorite Story* because of what He does in the most hostile conditions. I know if He can do something so striking there, He can make Himself known in my life as well. May you encounter Him in His power as you walk with the Master.

1

THE GREATEST SERMON EVER, PART I

> And seeing the multitudes, He went up on a mountain, and when He was seated His disciples came to Him. Then He opened His mouth and taught them, saying: "Blessed are the poor in spirit, for theirs is the kingdom of heaven. Blessed are those who mourn, For they shall be comforted. Blessed are the meek, for they shall inherit the earth. Blessed are those who hunger and thirst for righteousness, for they shall be filled. Blessed are the merciful, for they shall obtain mercy. Blessed are the pure in heart, for they shall see God. Blessed are the peacemakers, for they shall be called sons of God. Blessed are those who are persecuted for righteousness' sake, for theirs is the kingdom of heaven.
>
> Blessed are you when they revile and persecute you, and say all kinds of evil against you falsely for My sake. Rejoice and be exceedingly glad, for great is your reward in heaven, for so they persecuted the prophets who were before you" (Matthew 5:1–12).

By operating in an amazing manner in the region, Jesus easily attracted huge crowds of people. During this entire season of ministry, He healed people, set men and women free from bondage, and did the essential works of ministry which marked His entire time of service (Matthew 4:23). It was also during this season of ministry that Jesus spent a full night in prayer and followed that prayer meeting with an act that forever changed the face of His ministry. He selected from the masses of people twelve men so that they could more closely follow Him. We call these men the Apostles. Jesus understood the times and knew it would not be long until He would need others to carry His message beyond the narrow confines of Israel. He met this challenge by His selection of the Twelve from among the larger group of followers.

Established and duly deputized, His band was soon equally hard-pressed by the multitudes of people. Jostled and harassed, Jesus and this small group of men retreated further into the surrounding hills. Once there, in something akin to a retreat, Jesus taught these men the basics of Kingdom living. You and I have come to call this the Sermon on the Mount.

It is worth noting that Matthew's account is much longer than that of Luke (6:20-49). Luke also set his story in a plain where Jesus spoke to a large crowd rather than the smaller gathering of disciples. For some this presents a problem. I have no problem grasping the idea that Jesus taught something as vital as these Kingdom principles more than once. I also have no problem understanding these stories were taught in various settings and that Luke omitted some of the more "Jewish" teachings in his treatise to a Gentile named Theophilus (1:3). At any rate, for our purposes, we are going to consider the fuller account of Matthew because it is the longest, and most comprehensive, set of teachings given by Jesus. This teaching is, in effect, the very ethic of the kingdom of God. If we want to know how to live in the Kingdom, dig in, for here it is.

Forget About Doctrine!

Let's agree on something upfront. It is not nearly as much fun to dig into what Jesus taught us as it is to examine what He can do for us. I do not become as excited when I delve into "salt and light" and how that will affect my everyday life as I do when I revel in the idea of Him speaking a word into my life situation and watching demonic forces flee. I doubt any of us do. Sadly, this has kept many of us snared by the demonic powers we despise when, had we given equal attention to His teachings, we would have been set free and learned how to walk out our victory.

Remember, they called Jesus "Rabbi," meaning He was a master *"Teacher"* (John 1:38). To hear Jesus presented by some people today, He is not much more than a wizard or illusionist who came only to perform the spectacular in people's lives. Make no mistake: He came for that purpose. He is here to snap the chains of bondage in the life of any who dares to call His name. But that is only one side of the equation. Jesus also taught us how to live out that victory.

I believe God is more interested in who we are than what we do. He wants to create in us more than a groveling, fear-induced obedience. He wants us to live out the Kingdom ethic. He wants far more than to do something in us and then plant us on a pew for sixty years. He wants us to become disciples. Learners. His followers.

Jesus knew there were masses of people who needed more than just healing or deliverance. The throngs needed someone to guide them into the life of the Kingdom, someone to point them in the right direction. He wanted more than simple healing for them. Healing fades over time in everyone who receives a miracle. He wanted more than a stomach-stretching meal for them. That meal, filling as it was, was gone in a few hours, and more food was needed. He wanted them to be strong in the doctrine of Heaven. He wanted them to constantly grow in power, able to deal with every attack Satan would launch. I am confident He desires nothing less for you and me.

As Jesus strolled up that hillside, His disciples in tow, it is easy to imagine the words of Isaiah rolling through His consciousness:

> In the last days the mountain of the Lord's temple will be established as the highest of the mountains; it will be exalted above the hills and all nations will stream to it. Many peoples will come and say, "Come, let us go up to the mountain of the Lord, to the temple of the God of Jacob. He will teach us his ways, so that we may walk in his paths." The law will go out from Zion, the word of the Lord from Jerusalem (Isaiah 2:2-3 NIV).

I think you and I should stream to that mountain. Not to shout, though shouting to the Lord is proper. We should flock there, eager to appear before the Master. Not to dance, even though dancing before the Lord is a delight to our Father. We should scurry to that craggy height. Not to exult in glee but to learn His ways and walk in His paths. There we will discover the glory that comes to those who give themselves completely to learning and following His commands.

Understanding the Sermon

Jesus, like all great teachers of His day, employed a method of teaching in which He would give a series of short statements followed by exposition and application. It was, and remains, an effective mode of communicating the truth.

To grasp the vast amount of teaching Jesus gave, I follow the idea that sets forth the notion Jesus laid out what we call the "Beatitudes" and then followed with an exposition on His life-changing teaching. To break this tasty meal into manageable bites, we will consider the sermon in this fashion: (1) The Believer and His Fellow Man: The Ethics of the Kingdom of God; (2) The Believer and His God: The Energy of the Kingdom of God.

Of course, every worthwhile sermon must have an introduction, a window that allows the light to shine on what follows. Jesus, being the Master Teacher, put this tactic on full display. In the Beatitudes, He had an agenda for the massive material He would deliver. Set in the mountains, this "apostolic retreat" was something I would have loved to attend. Imagine having the Son of God there, within easy reach, teaching you firsthand the principles of the Kingdom. How staggering would it have been to have been in that number and had time to ask the Master Teacher of the universe questions regarding the depths of His words! Being present would have been the most glorious moment of learning in the history of humanity. Alas, we must limit ourselves to studying what has been passed down to us as well as the ideas which percolated from His words. Such action is thrilling, but I can hardly wait until I get to chat with Him in person.

The Foundation of the Kingdom: The Beatitudes

Jesus started simple. He laid out a foundation of what it means to be in the kingdom of Heaven. If you pay any attention to the thrust of His message, one thing stands out. Jesus intends for His followers to be joyful souls. If you don't believe me, look closely for yourself. Notice how many times the word *blessed* occurs. No less than nine times in this short setting (Matthew 5:1-11), Jesus said, "These are happy people." That's what the word *blessed* means. Joyful. Happy. Of course, it runs much deeper than the shallowness of our current understanding of being happy. The ancient Greeks used this same word to describe the isle of Cyprus. They viewed that paradise as such a wonderful place, so fertile, so serene, so calm and alluring, that a person could move there and never have to venture beyond her shores to find all they would ever want. That's what Jesus set before us. He described a way of life so complete, so fulfilling, so rewarding that we do not have to turn to the happiness of this world to be satisfied.

Contrast that with the meaning of our modern word *happiness*. It comes from the root word which means "happenstance." The world's happiness is based on whatever happens to come our way. If a good day happens to us, we are happy. If a good mood prevails, we are happy. Conversely, if the opposite occurs, and it often does, our lives are marked by sadness. Let's be honest. If we go to an amusement park and it rains, we act like the world has fallen apart. Jesus wants to instill something much deeper, of greater substance, in us than such shallow and fickle moodiness. He is not interested in creating in us a superficial ebullience that is dependent on the passing fads of the day. He is letting us in on a secret that most humanity misses completely. We can find joy and real happiness, even when life deals us the bitterest blows.

This contradiction is evident from the outset of His teaching. Jesus began where all true spiritual life is initiated by laying out the blessings of a proper relationship with the Father.

> *"Blessed are the poor in spirit, for theirs is the Kingdom of Heaven"* (Matthew 5:3).

The idea that one can be simultaneously poor and happy flies in the face of modern thinking. The mantra constantly beaten into our spirit is to grab all we can get and hoard it. The idea of "he who dies with the most toys wins" dies hard in modern America. Still, what Jesus taught then and still calls for today is true. The only way to true happiness with God begins with the self-discovery of our poverty.

This is not a form of self-loathing. Nor is it a path that leads to self-destructive behavior. This poverty is a realization of how destitute we are without God. It is a recognition of how lost and utterly devoid of God's goodness we happen to be. We cannot be saved without coming to grips with this sobering truth. The truth of our alienation from God and our dependence on Christ must dawn on us to bring us to Him and ultimately make it to Heaven.

Perhaps this is one reason so many strong-willed, self-made people have trouble coming to the Cross. Such individuals are self-reliant, strong, and capable, and, in many cases, they have survived because of their wit and street smarts. To them, receiving the Word of God like a trusting little child runs contrary to every animalistic instinct. Yet, such a mindset is required, according to Jesus (Matthew 18:3).

Once we grasp our inability to survive without the provision of the Kingdom, we can lay a foundation for a successful life to be built. Our poverty opens for us an inexhaustible fountain of supply. All the resources, forgiveness, and provisions ever needed are available. It is the supreme oxymoron: *The less we have, the more we have*. Yet that is the way the Kingdom works. Get this one right and every need in life is matched by the endless supply of God's never-ending Kingdom.

> *"Blessed are those who mourn, for they shall be comforted"* (Matthew 5:4).

Happiness and mourning mix like water and oil—until you look at what Jesus was teaching. The word He used for *mourning* is extreme. It is the excessive, expressive mourning that accompanies the loss of a dear loved one. Through the years, I have witnessed hundreds of funerals and stood with grieving families as they walked through a time of mourning. Like you, I have stood there and looked at the remains of a loved one and mourned. I have grieved over my loss.

In this case, I don't think Jesus was talking about dead people. I think Jesus was building on His previous statement about poverty. This is mourning over the utter spiritual bankruptcy that possessed us. I contend this is repentance for the that has destroyed us. It is brokenness over the spiritual poverty that has stripped us of dignity and standing with God.

Jesus was saying that broken, messy, weeping repentance over our sin brings comfort from Heaven. I know that is not very popular in today's church. Most churches will usher you out of the auditorium if you start sobbing out loud. However, it was not your favorite teacher but Jesus who set this in motion. This correlates well with the whole of God's Word, where we discover how poverty before God was met with blubbering sobs of men and women who cried out to Him for help. Listen to the psalmist describe his emotional reaction, his mourning over the brokenness of people due to sin: *"Rivers of water run down from my eyes, because men do not keep your law"* (Psalm 119:136).

Ezekiel, while looking at a time when sinfulness was rampant, spoke about the blessedness of mourning over the tragic sins of the culture: *"The Lord said to him, 'Go through the midst of the city, through the midst of Jerusalem, and put a mark on the foreheads of the men who sigh and cry over the abominations that are done within it'"* (Ezekiel 9:4).

Those far from what you and I would label "good church people" are known to mourn over the sinfulness that has wrecked their lives:

> A woman in the city who was a sinner, when she knew that Jesus sat at the table in the Pharisee's house, brought an alabaster flask of fragrant oil, and stood at His feet behind Him weeping; and she began to wash His feet with her tears, and wiped them with the hair of her head; and she kissed His feet and anointed them with the fragrant oil (Luke 7:37-38).

Those close to Jesus also demonstrated the ability to become broken over sinful proclivities. *"When Simon Peter saw it, he fell down at Jesus' knees, saying, 'Depart from me, for I am a sinful man, O Lord'"* (Luke 5:8).

These, along with many other passages, set the stage for those who are willing to mourn over their poverty. When it finally hits us how utterly sinful and how completely unlike God we are, it produces emotions similar to when a loved one dies. It hurts. It aches. It keeps us awake at night. It gnaws at us, and we weep until we have no more tears left to spill. In fact, the older I get, the more pronounced this becomes. I realize how completely lost I am without Christ.

What happens next? Condemnation? Judgment? Hellfire and brimstone? No, not at all. Those who dare to be so open and vulnerable before God are given something totally unexpected. Rather than scathing condemnation, we are given the comfort of hearing "forgiven." Far from hearing a laundry list of wrongs we've committed, we are comforted by hearing "paid in full." Even when the accuser berates us, we hear echoing through the annals of time, "nailed to the cross."

As Jesus continued to demonstrate the differences in the Kingdom of Heaven and the kingdoms of this world, He uttered a statement that is, perhaps, one of the most misunderstood statements in Scripture:

> *"Blessed are the meek, for they shall inherit the earth"* (Matthew 5:5).

What image pops into your mind when you hear *meek*? Many of us immediately conjure up a pasty-faced, spineless runt who allows everyone to walk over him. You know that person, don't you? Moving about with their head hanging down, always bowing to the whims and criticisms of others. We have come to equate being fearful and beaten down with meekness. Thankfully, that image and the real meaning of Jesus' term are opposites.

Bible scholar William Barclay delved into how Aristotle defined the term: "the mean between excessive anger and excessive angerlessness." It is a happy medium between too much and too little. Barclay translated Jesus' statement as "Happy is the man who is always angry at the right time and never angry at the wrong time."[1]

The classical usage of this word includes the image of the mighty steed, prepped and eager for battle. The horse is ready, primed, anticipating the battle for which it was born. Adrenalin surges through every fiber of the mighty beast. He is ready and willing to charge. Still, this mighty animal is completely under the control and constraint of the rider. He submits his might to the will of the saddle's occupant. Another image is a powerful dog that has been domesticated. Large, powerful, and capable of inflicting great damage and even death, he is nonetheless

---

[1] William Barclay, *The Daily Bible Study Series: Matthew* (Philadelphia: Westminster Press, 1975), 96.

a part of the family. He plays with the children, allowing them to ride on his back, pull on his ears, and tug on his tail. Yet, in a flash, he will rise to defend those same children with all his might, even to the death.

That, my friend, is meekness. Strength under control. Power under restraint. Moses was called *"very meek, above all the men which were on the face of the earth"* (Numbers 12:3). But he was not a weak guy who was afraid to lead or frightened to make a decision. He was well aware of the glory of the Lord being on him, but he refused to flaunt that power for his self-aggrandizement. That is meekness personified.

Another aspect of meekness is teachability. The meek among us are fully aware of their lack and their need. Their meekness is displayed in their expression of their poverty before God. They are hungry to be made better, never satisfied with their status with God. Perhaps that is where James was aiming when he called believers to live a life where we *"receive with meekness the implanted word, which is able to save your souls"* (James 1:21).

Jesus promises those who are willing to become meek before Him the inheritance of the earth. There is a sense in which that is true today. Those who are restrained and under control are given great trust. We allow them to manage wealth, which is staggering. We entrust them with immense power—power that can destroy life on our planet. But Jesus went further. A day is coming when those who dare to bow before Him and bring themselves under His discipline will inherit a new heaven and earth, prepared especially for those who surrender to His lordship.

Then, as if to throw the car in reverse, Jesus shifted direction.

> *"Blessed are those who hunger and thirst for righteousness, for they shall be filled"* (Matthew 5:6).

We often find ourselves in direct contradiction with the Kingdom. We take the meek and try to make them mice when God intends them to be powerful steeds. Then we turn around and take spiritual hunger, which God intends to be that of a sumo wrestler, and try to put everyone on a spiritual starvation program. Jesus set a tone that very few grasp. Being New Testament believers, we tend to think of this as the thing Christ gives us in place of our sinfulness through His work on the cross. But this goes a little further than that. This righteousness stretches to our behavior and motives. Simply put, this is a life eaten up with being pleasing to God. This is not what gets us saved. That's the righteousness Christ imparts. This is the life we lead after salvation. It is the life we give daily to Jesus, hungering for Him and His way in every aspect of our journey.

Let's be honest. So many of us get discontented and unhappy. Even as I peck away on this keyboard, there are stories of well-known worship leaders and ministers walking away from the faith. People are shaken up that such prominent people have abandoned their faith. They wonder, *What in the world happened? How could they possibly walk away?* The answer is right before our eyes. Jesus said happiness and contentment are found in a constant search for a life-change pleasing to the Father!

The formula is simple. We are told to "hunger and thirst." Jesus used two everyday occurrences to show us how passionate our pursuit of God should be. Both are perpetual events. It really doesn't matter how much we eat today; hunger will come back around tomorrow. We can drink a gallon of water today, but tomorrow, we will be thirsty again.

Pause a moment and think about your favorite holiday. Thanksgiving. Christmas. Fourth of July. Whichever day you love to celebrate. How many times have you, on that particular day, eaten so much that you thought, *I am about to pop! I will never eat again!* Then, sheepishly, a few hours later, you slip into the kitchen to raid the fridge for a "little snack." Jesus tells us that kind of hunger for pleasing God will bring true happiness into our lives.

Psalm 42:1-2 describes it like this: *"As the deer pants for the water brooks, so pants my soul for You, O God. My soul thirsts for God, for the living God. When shall I come and appear before God?"* The psalmist compared his thirst for God to a deer in the wilderness longing for water. This is not a passing fancy; it is a thirst that must be quenched. The only thing capable of satisfying the deer's thirst is the cool waters that flow from the springs. Likewise, the only thing that will bring real happiness and contentment into our lives is the close and revealed presence of the living God. Oh, that we could thirst so for Him that we would not be denied! Here is a great promise for those who whet their appetite for Him: There is more than enough to go around. Jesus said we would be gorged, filled to satiation. Not a snack. Not a candy bar to get us through. A banquet set before us filled with more than we could devour in ten sittings.

Of course, those who are content will step back and state their satisfaction with things as they are. They will say, "There is no need for all that fuss. Jesus gave me all I will ever need when He saved me." I won't argue with you. Stay as you are, and enjoy your journey. But before you decide to walk the rest of your sojourn here thin as a rail, consider one more question: *What happens when you eat too much?* You know the answer. It is the most distasteful word in the English vocabulary. You get fat!

I have worked all my life against getting fat. If you know me, you can go ahead and say it: "You should have worked more!"

I get it. But this is a different matter. I want to gorge on the righteousness of God and get fat like Santa. In fact, I want to become a righteousness-of-God sumo wrestler! Want to know why? Isaiah 10:27 says, *"In that day their burden will be lifted from your shoulders, their yoke from your neck; the yoke will be broken because you have grown so fat"* (NIV).

Some versions state we break the yoke with the anointing. Either way, the message is clear. Like the ox that eventually snaps the yoke that once held him captive, we can become so filled and large with God's righteous anointing that no weapon our enemy decides to use against us will prevail. We will discover, rising within us, a mighty river of His anointing that will obliterate every hindrance Satan can place before us. Oh, to be so filled with Christ and His glory!

From focusing on our relationship with the Father, Jesus turned His focus to becoming Kingdom-like in our relationships with others. In Matthew 5, verse seven naturally follows verse six. If you are blitzing through the statements of Jesus, you might not notice the shift in focus. Up to this point, Jesus was talking about the relationship between us and God. The next few verses, however, start to get a little sticky.

Now, Jesus informs us what is required in our dealings with each other. This is the stuff we will face at the final exam, so we better sit up and pay attention as Jesus outlines how we should live with each other *here* to live with Him *there*! It begins with a mindset glaringly absent in many churches today.

> *"Blessed are the merciful, for they shall obtain mercy"* (Matthew 5:7).

This is a simple principle: *God treats us like we treat others.* In this case, if we want mercy, we must show mercy. It sounds easy until we try living out what Jesus meant.

From a Biblical standpoint, *mercy* goes beyond feeling sorry for someone or not striking back when you can legitimately do so. It carries the notion of getting inside someone's skin to see through their eyes and feel as they do. It means doing your best to understand what makes someone tick and what causes them to act as they do.

Honestly, I don't want to do that. I am too busy with myself to put that much energy into understanding you. After all, I want to occupy my mind with what you did and said and how it affects me. I want to spend my time being sullen over how you acted and how it upset me. I am far too busy nursing my anger to stop and consider what is happening in your life.

Sound familiar? We all have those seasons where we are much too interested in our own way to do what Jesus called on us to do. Still, this demand from Jesus calls us to stop living life just for ourselves and stop pouting and nursing a grudge toward others. We must invest in their lives to understand why they are acting that way

I love a story Steven Covey relates in his classic book, *Seven Habits of Highly Effective People.* He talks about riding on a bus where some young kids were going nuts. They were crawling all over the place, jumping up and down, intruding into his space. To make matters worse, the father sat dazed and unmoved by his raucous and aggravating kids. While his children climbed all over other passengers, he was sitting in a trance, oblivious to their manic activity. Things got so bad that Covey got the father's attention and told him his children were making a scene. The father, shaken to reality by his rebuke, apologized. In a shaky voice, he told Covey he had just left the hospital, the kids in tow, where their mother had died a few moments before. He told Covey, "None of them really knew how to act in that moment." Ouch!

Jesus calls us to stop living like we are the center of the universe. He wants us to realize what happens to others might have an adverse effect on them. He calls us to surrender the idea that our opinion is all that matters. He demands that we come down from the mountain of our personal lordship and see how life really functions. As I pointed out earlier, the deeper we get into the Beatitudes, the more we will rush back to the first one about being impoverished before God, and the more we will realize how much we need the ample forgiveness found in the Kingdom. Here's the beauty of this demand of Jesus. The more we grant mercy, the more mercy we will find. I am thrilled that His mercies are never exhausted. I rejoice in the fact they are renewed with the dawn of each new day in my life (Lamentations 3:23).

Let's move on. Jesus digs even deeper into our interactions with one another.

> *"Blessed are the pure in heart, for they shall see God"* (Matthew 5:8).

The word *pure* was used for clothes that had been washed or an army that had been cleared of dissidents and deserters. It meant something was clean and ready for ultimate use.

For those who think Jesus set a standard that eradicated the need for inner purity and holiness and that He considers all such teachings legalism, stop and take a closer look. While the Pharisees called for a focus only on the outward, Jesus set a new standard by telling us it was not enough to be ceremonially pure. He became totally radical in His claim. We are to be pure to the core of our being.

Consider this inner purity in light of the previous provision of happiness given by the Lord. When it comes to showing mercy, it is possible to withhold doing something harmful or exacting revenge while at the same time harboring intense hatred for the one to whom outward mercy was shown. Oh yes, we all know what it is like not to hurl the insult and withhold the scathing rebuke, only to walk away seething with anger. Jesus calls for more than "not hitting them back." He says you and I have to forgive people completely. We have to do it deep within, from our souls.

This is the most difficult thing we are called on to do in our Christian walk. This demand for deep, inner purity can never be attained without a constant pursuit of all that Heaven offers and the utter abandonment of our carnal pursuits. But the glorious part is such a life enables us to see God.

Those who embrace this purity will one day see God. Like Job, who in his utter desperation made the faith-laced claim that he would one day see God for himself (Job 19:26), those who chase after God in this fashion will one day cast their eyes upon the Lord. But there is another aspect to "seeing" God found here. It can mean to "perceive." In other words, those who give themselves to this purity, this inner readiness to all God wants from them, put themselves in a position to perceive what God is doing and saying. God makes Himself known to the pure in heart.

On the heels of that amazing call, Jesus issued another demand that even the most corrupt men on earth recognize today.

> *"Blessed are the peacemakers, for they shall be called the sons of God"* (Matthew 5:9).

Our world honors peacemakers. We elevate them, granting them great status. We even have the Nobel Peace Prize, which highlights those who supposedly work toward peace. A look at some of the recipients will give you pause, but that's another story. The fact is, we are most God-like when we are striving for peace, laboring for peace among people. The reason peacemakers stand out so much in our current culture is because there are so few of them. I think the words of General Omar Bradley, himself a man of war and death, had to say in a Memorial Day speech in 1948 still apply to our culture: "We have too many men of science, too few men of God. We have grasped the mystery of the atom and rejected the Sermon on the Mount. . . . Ours is a world of nuclear giants and ethical infants. We know about more war than we know about peace and more about killing than we know about living."[2]

Bradley was right. Our culture knows more about death than how to have peace. Jesus calls on us, His church, to be peacemakers. Notice He did not call on us to be peace-lovers, though that is included. We are to be creators of peace.

There are times when one arrives at peace by turning the other cheek. Most people take that immediate line of thinking when pondering this idea. Some want to take this command and make every believer a doormat or a weakling who is always on the receiving end of every wrong. They are not going to call one such as that a peacemaker. They are going to call that person a wimp.

There is also a time when you are a peacemaker because you are strong enough to confront and deal with an issue. If you are in an abusive family situation, you are not making peace by allowing abusive behavior to continue; you are enabling the abuser to exist unchecked. If a nation bows to another nation

---

[2] *Illustrating the Gospel of Matthew*, James Hightower, compiler (Nashville: Broadman, 1982), 26.

intent on its destruction and never rises to meet the challenge, it is not making peace; it is setting the table for destruction. Our call is to make peace, to mediate, to go between, and to help reconcile. That can get dicey—getting caught between two warring parties—but that is what Christ calls for us to do. All of which leads to the final happiness Jesus mentioned. If ever there was a seeming contradiction, this one certainly takes top billing.

> *"Blessed are those who are persecuted for righteousness' sake, for theirs is the Kingdom of Heaven. Blessed are you when they revile and persecute you, and say all kinds of evil against you falsely for My sake. Rejoice and be exceedingly glad, for great is your reward in heaven, for so they persecuted the prophets who were before you"* (Matthew 5:10-12).

One of the fascinating aspects of the ministry of Jesus, and one which seems to be absent from today's mega-ministries and celebrity ministers, is the utter honesty He employed when describing what the true believer would encounter. Let's be honest: If Jesus were around today and trying to start a church in typical America, He would not be sugar-coating His claims, promising a greater life, a more fulfilling job, and indeed a better *everything*. Instead, Jesus would let folks know this is not about their comfort but their character.

He just finished teaching that making peace would result in His followers being called "*sons of God.*" He then added while they were out there making peace, people were going to be shooting at them. Even when we are out there doing our best, trying to carry the message of His love to a dying world, we will catch it from people who do not believe and do not want others to believe.

Within a short span of time, Jesus' original disciples fully understood what He meant. They were treated in horrific manners beyond description. The way the early church was treated, it's a wonder there is still a church at all. But something about Jesus was so powerful, so intoxicating, even the pangs of torturous death could not extinguish the church's passion for Him.

Mark this, Jesus said trouble was coming *"for righteousness' sake."* Remember, He said earlier that those who were obsessed with seeking His righteousness in this life would be filled. The oddity of this promise is the more of His righteousness we seek and obtain, the more we will be disliked by the world. The more of Him we receive, the greater the rejection will be. Even now, the dark clouds of persecution are growing over the church in America. It's coming; we better get ready.

When it comes, let's make sure it isn't because of our silliness. There has been far too much junk on the airwaves and in the arenas. Let's make sure it isn't because of our sullenness. We have been too hard on sinners, treating them harshly, even though we have done our fair share of sinning. Instead, let's see persecution come because the church is spending millions feeding hungry people or investing in downtrodden neighborhoods and turning them around, all the while having nothing but the name of Jesus emblazoned on what we are doing. Let's start laying hands on the sick once more to see them healed. Let's have enough of His glory present in our gatherings that addicts are set free and enough care that we disciple them into mature believers. Let's do all that, not for one ounce of glory for "our church" or "our denomination," but for His glory!

Make no mistake. When that happens, the enemy will arise. He always does. Satan's attacks will be personal and intense. At that moment, you and I are called to act like radicalized zealots for the Kingdom. Jesus said when all that happens, rejoice! Jump up and down for joy that they persecute us. Strange. Yet such actions on our part place us in good company. Prophets have been treated like that for millennia. God's servants have been assaulted throughout the ages. We are simply part of the line of those whom God will someday point toward and utter, "Well done!" Being part of what He unfolds will be ample reward for living out His teachings.

SERMON OUTLINE

Introduction: As Jesus ministered in the might of the Spirit, He attracted huge crowds. As the masses grew, He pulled aside twelve men who were called to walk more closely with Him. These twelve we call Apostles. Like the Master, the crowds pressed into them and Jesus knew the time was coming when they would be left to carry on His mission. They retreated with Jesus, who taught them extensively about the Kingdom.

Matthew is more exhaustive in his account than Luke, and for some, that is a problem. However, common sense tells us Jesus taught these Kingdom principles on more than one occasion and location. If we want to live out life in Kingdom style, dig in, for here is the greatest sermon ever preached.

1. FORGET ABOUT DOCTRINE!
    a. Digging In
    b. Developing Disciples
    c. Discovering Glory
2. FORMULATING HIS SERMON
    a. Method of Teaching
    b. Massive Material: Beatitudes
    c. Master on Display
3. FOUNDATION OF THE KINGDOM
    a. Blessed Regardless
    b. Blessings with God
        i. Spiritual Poverty
        ii. Spiritual Mourning
        iii. Spiritual Meekness
        iv. Spiritual Hunger

c. Becoming Kingdom-like with Others
   i. Required Mercy
   ii. Required Purity
   iii. Required Peacemaking
   iv. Required Persecution

Conclusion: The amazing part of the first segment of Jesus' sermon is that He lets us know the more we seek Him, the more hostile our world will become. Darkness and light will not dwell together, so we must not be upset by what we see today. Even as things worsen, we are part of a long line of strong believers who endured until the end and witnessed His ultimate salvation. We must hold on, knowing the words "Well done" will come at the end of the day.

STUDY QUESTIONS

1. Why would Matthew include more details than Luke? Can you explain the different points of emphasis? Do you think it is plausible Jesus taught Kingdom principles on more than one occasion?
2. What do you think are the distinguishing marks of one who is an apprentice to Jesus?
3. Explain what it means to live the "blessed" life.
4. How is it possible for one to be poor and yet blessed? How can mourning result in blessings? Are the meek more than doormats? Do you hunger enough for His righteousness to be filled?
5. What are some differences between how Jesus teaches us to relate to God and people? Do you

feel mercy, purity, peacemaking, and persecution are requirements or suggestions? How do we demonstrate these qualities to others?

6. Can you point to persecution in our country? How do you plan on responding when you are forced to make a choice that results in persecution?

2

THE GREATEST SERMON EVER, PART II

"You are the salt of the earth; but if the salt loses its flavor, how shall it be seasoned? It is then good for nothing but to be thrown out and trampled underfoot by men. You are the light of the world. A city that is set on a hill cannot be hidden. Nor do they light a lamp and put it under a basket, but on a lampstand, and it gives light to all who are in the house. Let your light so shine before men, that they may see your good works and glorify your Father in heaven.

"Do not think that I came to destroy the Law or the Prophets. I did not come to destroy but to fulfill. For assuredly, I say to you, till heaven and earth pass away, one jot or one tittle will by no means pass from the law till all is fulfilled. Whoever therefore breaks one of the least of these commandments, and teaches men so, shall be called least in the kingdom of heaven; but whoever does and teaches them, he shall be called great in the kingdom of heaven. For I say to you, that unless your righteousness exceeds the righteousness of the scribes and Pharisees, you will by no means enter the kingdom of heaven" (Matthew 5:13–20).

As we continue with the attempt to plumb the depths of the greatest sermon ever preached, the temptation is to stop, dig in, and seek to mine out the last ounce of truth from every word that fell from the Master's lips. Such an aspiration would lead to years, even decades, of study and, in the case of the preacher, vast amounts of preaching and teaching material. Still, how can we not stop and ponder these words? How is it possible we have tossed these words aside, giving them only an occasional passing glance? What is wrong with us when we speed read through these words, searching for something more "relevant" to our situation? After all, Jesus himself—not your favorite preacher—is declaring here what it means to be part of His Kingdom. These might be the most important words we encounter in the entire New Testament. These teachings should consume us. They should occupy our thoughts every day. In fact, to say we should become obsessed with these words is an understatement.

Why should we become so carried away with these few verses? The challenge offered by Jesus in this setting gives ample reason for taking His words so seriously: *"For I say to you, that unless your righteousness exceeds the righteousness of the scribes and Pharisees, you will by no means enter the kingdom of heaven"* (Matthew 5:20).

That one statement jumps off the page like something written in all caps and bold print. We need to once again pay attention because this is Heaven and hell stuff. We need to pay attention because this is our exit exam. I want to pass that grand exam, don't you?

Make no mistake about this: Christ's church is not all it should be. If your task today is to point out the inconsistencies within the body, it does not take an exhaustive search. If your goal is to find my inadequacies, to chat with others about my deficiencies, you will be provided with ample material. I have shortages in my life that are readily evident. If your goal is to search for proof that we, the church, are not all we should be and then use that as a reason not to follow the perfect Galilean, it won't take you long to decide against following Jesus. But before you launch out on your own, consider what one person said about the staggering mess that occupied Noah's ark. He quipped, "If it were not for all the trouble outside, I would not be able to stand the stench on the inside."

That sums it up. You can pick your poison. Float with the rest of us less-than-perfect within the church or drown with a godless culture. I plan to stay in the boat.

Pictures of the Christian Life

Jesus used a couple of powerful metaphors to describe His followers in this present evil world. Both terms, *salt* and *light*, carry a vast array of applications and call for us to stand out in the darkness around us.

When Jesus called us *"salt"* (Matthew 5:13), He spoke about something familiar to people worldwide. Salt is an integral part of our lives, and we cannot live without it. Most Americans take in too much, largely due to a highly processed diet. Still, if you eliminate it altogether, you can develop a sickness called "hyponatremia," which can create a laundry list of nasty effects and even lead to death. Salt is essential, and Jesus used this common, everyday material to let us know how we should to affect those around us.

For instance, salt is a preservative. It was and is still used to protect and save meat from spoilage in regions where refrigeration either does not exist or is in short supply. Using a copious amount of salt, meat can be rubbed or dipped in a brine solution, and it will remain edible for a much longer period of time than if left unprotected. In just that fashion, believers "salt" society, keeping it from utter ruin and destruction. We know from Scripture that our influence will not prevent the final, utter ruination of this earth.[1] Still, our task is to preserve all that is possible and bring them to Christ.

Salt also serves as a flavoring instrument. Those things in the store labeled "sodium-free" are costly because they only sell a limited quantity. The producers of those products cannot afford to employ a mass production and sales method. People don't flock to the stores to buy them. Why? Because salt-free chips and bread are not as tasty as those same products containing sodium. Salt does something to food that we like. It enhances the flavor. It brings the best to the surface. That's what you and I are supposed to be doing, bringing the very best to the surface.

Likewise, when Jesus referred to us as *"light"* (Matthew 5:14-16), He spoke about something well aware to every person alive and equipped with sight. Light illumines darkness. Light makes clear what is obscured and hidden.

You and I live in a very dark and secretive world system. All around us, the powers of darkness do their best to cover up, hinder, and hide the truth. Listen to the newscasts of the two polemically different reporting systems, and it is clear someone is lying!

Why is this the case? Why does it seem no one tells the whole truth? It is because the whole world—including governments, businesses, and social groups—is under the sway of the evil one (1 John 5:19). Since Satan is a liar at heart (John 8:44), one of his major tactics is to create a lying culture. Lies exist in the

[1] 2 Peter 3:10 informs us this earth will be utterly renovated with the fire of God's judgment.

darkness. It is hard to back up lies when light is shed on the matter. That's why Jesus is revolutionary when He shows up and tells us, "You are to be light, clearly pointing the way to Heaven through all the murky and dark lies being told around you!"

When I look at my calling and I seem to be born with an inbred dimmer switch, I wonder how I can possibly be a light pointing people to Jesus. After all, with all the foibles present in my life, how can I possibly direct others to the true Light? It is then, just before I reach the point of despair, I take a closer look at His statement in John 8:12: *"I am the light of the world. He who follows Me shall not walk in darkness but have the light of life."*

He is the light. I am but the reflection of His brilliance. If you wander outside on a clear night when the moon is full and bright in the sky, it seems like that white orb is bathing the landscape with its brilliance. Of course, the moon has no light of its own. It is simply reflecting the light radiating from the sun. I may not have light in me, but I can radiate the glory of Christ's presence in my life.

Put together, salt and light create a powerful picture of how we should relate to each other. Our task is to be salty—to be so powerful in our life following Jesus that we make others thirst for what we have. Our task is also to be brilliant—to shine in dark places, emitting the glory of what He has done in us so that people trapped in darkness can see the difference in those who follow Christ.

Years back, after a hurricane had swept into the Gulf Coast of Alabama, there were relief efforts galore. However, after the glitz of the cameras had moved to the next news cycle, a member of the church I was privileged to pastor, Joe Stewart, was still helping people get through the storm's devastation. I received a call from someone Joe had helped. This woman cried as she told me about his work—how he kept cleaning up and moving debris. In fact, she bragged about Joe so much I finally asked her to send me a picture of the guy to be sure we were talking about the same man. Just kidding!

That unchurched, far-from-Jesus woman was touched not by someone getting in her face and telling her what a sinner she happened to be. No great evangelist preached her a message on late-night television. She was not even affected by some relief agency that blew into town after the storm. Instead, that lady and her family were deeply impacted by a simple man who let his light shine and salted those people with the goodness of Jesus.

I am convinced that in the United States with churches galore, this will be the method of reaching people for Christ that produces real results. America has been soaked in the Gospel. Sure, there are plenty who have not heard, but they pass churches every day and have no desire to join us. We are not going to out-argue those people. We are not going to out-debate those convinced we are delusional. We are not going to coerce those adamantly opposed to the Gospel. We cannot scare them, trick them, nor advertise them into the Kingdom. If we are going to be effective, we must outlive them. Not in terms of years, but in this business of salt and light.

Jesus became straightforward with His comments about our lives. He does not mince words about our conduct among our fellow travelers on this journey. He declared, *"You are the salt of the earth; but if the salt loses it flavor, how shall it be seasoned? It is then good for nothing but to be thrown out and trampled underfoot by men. You are the light of the world. A city that is set on a hill cannot be hidden"* (Matthew 5:13-14).

Many of us seem to have forgotten we are part of a Kingdom, and this Kingdom has a King. We have difficulty with this concept because we are men and women who breathe *liberty!* We have free speech in this country, so we can say what we want. Nobody is going to tell us what to do! While those concepts may be true in America, they are becoming less true all the time . . . and they are not necessarily facts in the Kingdom. If you have fallen bankrupt before Jesus and pleaded your case of poverty (see the first Beatitude), you are no longer the one in charge.

Paul said we in the Kingdom have dual citizenship (Philippians 3:20). My citizenship registered in Heaven outranks the one I have here in the U.S. If you think less of me because of that statement, remember I have the right to say it! (Just kidding.) The truth remains, however, that my citizenship here will cease when I draw my last breath. My citizenship there is everlasting. That being the case, I better make sure of my "call and election" (2 Peter 1:10).

Some will argue, "But I thought the Cross took care of all that!" Relax. On the cross, Jesus did take care of the Law of God. He said, *"Do not think that I came to destroy the Law or the Prophets. I did not come to destroy but to fulfill. For assuredly, I say to you, till heaven and earth pass away, one jot or one tittle will by no means pass from the law till all is fulfilled"* (Matthew 5:17-18).

Jesus had to be sinless because the Law demanded it. Those millions of lambs slaughtered in sacrifice had to be perfect. No blemishes or spots. No imperfections allowed. In like manner, Jesus had to live without sin. That's why the Virgin Birth is such a big deal. Since Jesus was formed by the Holy Spirit in Mary's womb, he was born without the sinful nature we have.

Jesus lived out a sinless, perfect life. He fulfilled the Law and now stands in my stead, offering His perfection in the place of my imperfection. That's one reason I keep running back to the opening of the Beatitudes. I want ever to remember my spiritual poverty to receive Christ's perfection.

All that is prophesied in the Old Testament that has not yet come to pass will take place. Jesus' statement about *"one jot or one tittle"* is so profound it staggers the imagination. These were two punctuation phrases used by Jesus to illustrate how thorough the Father is about completing His Word.

The word *"jot"* is the Hebrew *yod*. It looks like an apostrophe. There are some 66,420 *yods* in the Hebrew Old Testament. The word *"tittle"* is the Hebrew serif. That is a tiny extension on some Hebrew letters which separates them from other letters in the alphabet. There are multiplied thousands of these tiny marks in the Old Testament. It would be like Jesus saying to us, "One dotting of an *i* or one crossing of a *t*." Can you imagine how many of those there are in the entire Old Testament? Just for fun, I counted the number of times there was a crossing of a *t* or dotting of an *i* in the first ten verses of Genesis 1. In the *New King James Version*, I came up with a total of 126 times in just the opening verses of the Bible. That is 126 times we are reminded how utterly reliable and trustworthy the Word of God is. Best of all, and this is the glorious part: *Jesus kept every bit of it for me!*

Naturally, we cannot be content to live within the confines of the Word. Hence, the rebellious nature of man is manifest when we utter, "So, I can live any way I want!" A dangerous thread of teaching in today's church is that a person can come to Christ, have a mighty conversion experience, and then return to the same sinful lifestyle that consumed them before meeting Jesus.

Such an idea makes as much sense as telling a newly married couple to live in sexual relationships with as many other partners as they wish because it will not harm their relationship. No one in their right mind would give that advice. Strangely enough, some teachers give that kind of advice to converts who come to Christ, ignoring the plain teaching of Scripture.

All we have to do is listen to Jesus in this great sermon.

> "Whoever therefore breaks one of the least of these commandments, and teaches men so, shall be called the least in the kingdom of heaven; but whoever does and teaches them, he shall be called great in the kingdom of heaven. For I say to you, that unless your righteousness exceeds the righteousness of the scribes and Pharisees, you will by no means enter the kingdom of heaven" (Matthew 5:19-20).

It seems to me Jesus contradicted Himself at this point. On one hand, He says breaking the commandments results not in eternal damnation, but in a reduction in rank in His Kingdom. Keeping the commandments and teaching others to do the same results in higher rank. In other words, break the commandments or keep them; it really does not have that much effect on the outcome. On the other hand, He points to the most scrupulous keepers of the Law on the planet, the Pharisees and scribes, and says unless we become more righteous than them, we don't have a chance of making it in. What gives?

I think Jesus was trying to make a point we sometimes miss. How we act is important. However, *why* we act how we act means more. Remember, Jesus pointed to a group of zealots who acted the part with great relish. They went to the Temple seven times every day. They prayed long prayers three times a day with some of those prayers lasting as long as two hours. They gave large sums of money to the church. They were masters at fasting, praying, tithing, church attendance, living a regulated life—all those things we think make someone "in" with God. Yet, Jesus pointed to them and said, "You have to have more than them even to make it in!"

So, can I live any way I want and be in the Kingdom? The short answer is a resounding "No!" How, then, do I know what is right and what is wrong? Hold on, Jesus still has a lot of teaching still to do about the proper Christian life. In fact, His next six teachings rock our world. If we will let them get deep into our spirit and begin to live as described by Jesus, it will be revolutionary. To say the adherence to these teachings will change our lives is the understatement of the century. A psychiatrist named James T. Fisher said:

> If you were able to take the sum total of all authoritative articles ever written by the most qualified of psychologists and psychiatrists on the subject of mental hygiene. . . . If you were to combine them and define them and leave out the excess verbiage. . . . If you were to take the whole of the meat and none of the parsley, and if you were to have these unadulterated bits of pure scientific knowledge concisely expressed by the most capable of living poets, you would have an awkward and incomplete summation of the Sermon on the Mount.[2]

I think Fisher could have used a bit of his own advice about cutting away the excess verbiage, but he makes a great point. This psychiatrist is telling the world we would all be happier

---

[2] Charles Swindoll, *Simple Faith* (Nashville: Thomas Nelson, 1991), 82-83

and lead more productive and effective lives if only we would employ what Jesus taught in the greatest sermon of all time.

Patterns of Christian Behavior

Jesus had much to say about murder. Our country is plagued with senseless, thoughtless, stupid slaughter. Everyone seems to point their fingers of blame at everyone else. Let's hear Jesus' words:

> "You have heard that it was said to those of old, 'You shall not murder, and whoever murders will be in danger of the judgment.' But I say to you that whoever is angry with his brother without a cause shall be in danger of the judgment. And whoever says to his brother, 'Raca!' shall be in danger of the council. But whoever says, 'You fool!' shall be in danger of hell fire. Therefore if you bring your gift to the altar, and there remember that your brother has something against you, leave your gift there before the altar, and go your way. First be reconciled to your brother, and then come and offer your gift. Agree with your adversary quickly, while you are on the way with him, lest your adversary deliver you to the judge, the judge hand you over to the officer, and you be thrown into prison. Assuredly, I say to you, you will by no means get out of there till you have paid the last penny" (Matthew 5:21–26).

Everyone standing around the Master understood He was talking about homicide. He was referencing the killing of innocent people. His teaching harkens back to the Old Testament and is rooted in the Ten Commandments (Exodus 20:13). We are not free to take human life at will. That extends to human life in the womb of a mother. The fact the world does not accept this as truth is bad enough. When the church moves in that direction, Heaven help us all!

Some religious people heard this and settled back, smug in their confidence they had never killed a person. I am sure some of them drifted mentally away, thinking, *This doesn't apply to me!* Then Jesus started dropping those "You have heard, but I say" bombs, and everyone was jolted from their chairs of ease. Jesus said we can be as guilty as if we murdered someone without ever laying a hand on them. Anger toward someone that gets out of hand results in the same judgment as murdering the person. He wants us to know our anger, left unchecked, will spiral downward and eventually wind up with us in dire straits before the Almighty. This is a seething anger, a brooding bitterness you nurse and keep alive. It is something which, unless brought under control through prayer, repentance, and surrender to the voice of the Holy Spirit, could lead to the taking of life.

I was once asked by a church member if we could meet for lunch. I agreed, and we met in a nice restaurant and had a pleasant meal. Since he and his wife were relatively new to the church, I engaged in the usual banter and tried to find out more about them. What he told me left me picking myself up off the floor. He confided how much he hated his wife. She was, in his assessment, a bossy, pushy, overbearing woman who made him miserable. Never mind they had been married more than forty years; he despised the ground she walked on. I was taken aback, but what he said next stunned me: "I have plotted and planned for many years how I could kill her." He went into detail about schemes where he could murder her, dispose of the body, and leave the country.

I went into my best pastoral stammering and told him he could never get away with it. If anything happened, I would know, and I would certainly tell the authorities. It never dawned on me he would have to do me in as well!

We left with me praying for him, and he told me he would not harm his wife—that he had laid it before the Lord and would forgive her. This man recently passed away, and his family, wife included, went on about what a gracious and loving man he was. If only she knew what I knew—that obituary and eulogy would have been different!

This man's attitude had put him in danger of going to hell even though he never committed the official act of murder. We must understand Jesus digs deeper than just "doing" something. He digs so deep that the entertainment of such a horrendous act places us in danger of judgment.

Jesus then said calling someone "*Raca*" placed a person in danger of standing before the council. This word means "empty-headed" or "worthless." In short, Jesus said when we "cuss somebody out," we stand in danger of judgment. In their world, that meant being excommunicated from the Temple. If you think, *Big deal, I don't like church that much anyway,* realize that being excommunicated from the Temple carried major economic and social repercussions. In our day, it would be like flinging some curse words at somebody who cut you off in traffic and then losing your job, your retirement, your house, and your friends—heavy stuff.

Jesus pressed deeper still. He said when we get so angry we dare to call someone "fool," we are in danger of going to hell. The word *fool* here is akin to our word "moron." The word in their culture meant considering someone totally worthless, deserving of eternal punishment, and unworthy of being saved.

Jesus was warning us about a downward spiral of anger and judgment that results in looking at someone and deciding they do not deserve to live. They are not worth the love of God, and we might as well turn our back on them and walk away.

The truth is simple but difficult to embrace. Jesus taught we do not have to shoot them to be guilty of murder. We can get so angry and become such a hothead that we decide they are not worthy of living. In so doing, we have already killed them in our hearts, which might lead us to kill them with our hands.

That's why Jesus taught us to settle our differences quickly. We must not let things fester. We must handle our conflicts with dispatch before we do something utterly foolish and wind up in court. Or worse yet, wind up standing condemned before God.

Here's how important this is: Jesus taught if we are in a worship service, and we realize someone has something against us, we are to make things right at that moment. We are not to pray about it for three weeks. We are not to rationalize about how right we are and how wrong they are. We are not to schedule an appointment with the pastor to discuss what we should do. We must stop doing what we are doing in church and make things right.

Think about all you do to get to church on Sunday. You get up, get cleaned up, drink some coffee, get the kids ready, have the obligatory fight on the way to church, get your offering ready, join in the singing, and focus on the sermon. However, Jesus says if someone has something against you, deal with it then. Not after church, then. Leave if you have to, but make things right.

Moving from murder, Jesus dove into a hot topic of His day and ours. He placed a demand on His followers about adultery, which is life-changing.

> "You have heard that it was said to those of old, 'You shall not commit adultery.' But I say to you that whoever looks at a woman to lust for her has already committed adultery with her in his heart. If your right eye causes you to sin, pluck it out and cast it from you; for it is more profitable for you that one of your members perish, than for your whole body to be cast into hell. And if your right hand causes you to sin, cut it off and cast it from you; for it is more profitable for you that one of your members perish, than for your whole body to be cast into hell" (Matthew 5:27–30).

They knew adultery was wrong. It had been pounded into their hearts and minds for centuries. Just like the prohibition against murder, this commandment was one of the "biggies" in the Ten Commandments given at Sinai (Exodus 20:14). Jesus validating this was no surprise to anyone in His audience. He then stepped into totally new territory and told them (and us in our sex-soaked culture) that when someone commits the act of adultery, they already committed the act in their heart long before any physical contact occurred. In other words, if we allow lust to build up in our hearts, we will commit sin long before there is ever a physical relationship. That is the reason we must be on guard and make sure we are continually coming back to the primary truth about righteous living. We are totally dependent on God and His resources to keep us strong.

Jesus was, in essence, stressing what the Old Testament had taught for centuries. The heart, the inner man, was guarded at all costs: *"Keep your heart with all diligence, for out it springs the issues of life"* (Proverbs 4:23). The issues we deal with today (and the laundry list is long), stem from heart issues. The struggles of our culture—racism, greed, violence—arise from the heart.

The answer, according to Jesus, is not found in governmental offices or the back seats of squad cars. The answer is found in the draconian approach He outlined regarding heart matters. Jesus said if there is an issue in our lives, we must deal with it swiftly and severely. His graphic language reveals how brutally we must confront our inner issues. If our eye offends us, cut it out! If our hand offends us, cut it off! If our foot offends us, amputate it.

Was Jesus being literal? I don't think so. A man can have an issue with lust and decide to have his eyes surgically removed. The problem is that lust is still embedded in his heart, and his imagination can run wild, even without eyesight. Jesus was using hyperbole to show the extremes to which we must go to steer clear of devastating sin.

However, the Master never suggested I actually cut anything off you. He never authorized you to sever anything off me. If you are not bothered by something that haunts me, pray for me, but don't try to be the instrument of correction. I will ultimately stand before the Lord on these issues. If I do what I must, everything will work out okay.

Jesus then turned to the issue of divorce, which He also addressed at other times. In Matthew 5:31-32, He declared: *"It has been said, 'whoever divorces his wife, let him give her a certificate of divorce.' But I say to you that whoever divorces his wife for any reason except sexual immorality causes her to commit adultery; and whoever marries a woman who is divorced commits adultery."* In Malachi 2:16, God said He *"hates divorce."* Let's settle that up front. In divorce, especially when children are present, no one wins except the lawyers. We must give serious thought to what Jesus said about this gut-wrenching process.

First, we need to understand the setting where this was spoken. The Romans divorced regularly, and the Jews had adopted a pattern much like their occupiers. The liberal teachings of Hillel allowed men to divorce for such trivial reasons as "burning dinner."[3] There is a reason you never read advice about women divorcing their husbands; they couldn't do it. The result was that men divorced their wives for virtually any perceived insult, often as a veil to cover their lustful pursuits.

They had twisted the Word of God to make it fit their carnal desires. Citing Moses as a commander of divorce, they made the Law say what they wanted it to say. Jesus corrected them, saying Moses "allowed" divorce only because of the hardness of men's hearts. In other words, divorce was never God's plan. It was granted because we, in our fallen state, were so obstinate that God allowed us this option.

We are not talking about adultery here. That was not the issue. There was a remedy for adultery in the Law of Moses, and it wasn't divorce. It was stoning! (Leviticus 20:10). Moses allowed divorce over things less serious than sexual immorality, but Jesus stood up and announced a new ethic. In the Kingdom, the only reason for divorce is immorality.

Let's step back from the red-hot issue and take a breath. Jesus did not say divorce is commanded; He said it is *"allowed."* The word He used indicates a lifestyle of action, not a single event. While divorce might be permitted if someone is unfaithful one time, that is not what this text demands. We need to pick this up and become serious again about divorce. We have wandered back into the morass into which the Jews ventured. Our modern day allows divorce for anything or nothing.

---

3 Mark E Moore, *The Chronological Life of Christ, Volume 2,* (Joplin, Missouri: College Press, 1997), 116.

God calls us to work through our differences and remain married. And, while divorce is something God hates, it is not the unpardonable sin. If sin has taken place through divorce, He will forgive the repentant person. However, if you are married and not getting along, work on it! Get on your face before God and cry out for His grace. Our world needs to see people who struggle as they cry out to God and receive His grace.

Since you and I live in an age where the truth is seldom heard, the fact Jesus is adamant about truth is particularly fitting.

> "Again you have heard that it was said to those of old, 'You shall not swear falsely, but shall perform your oaths to the Lord.' But I say to you, do not swear at all: neither by heaven, for it is God's throne; nor by the earth, for it is His footstool; nor by Jerusalem, for it is the city of the great King. Nor shall you swear by your head, because you cannot make one hair white or black. But let your 'Yes' be 'Yes,' and your 'No,' 'No.' For whatever is more than these is from the evil one" (Matthew 5:33–37).

Jesus harkened back to an Old Testament teaching about telling the truth. He used a concept they were familiar with to reiterate something they already knew: God's people are supposed to do what they say they will do, regardless. They understood this concept very well. If one of them said, "I swear by the temple," they were asserting their word was as sound and pure as that represented by the temple. It is akin to us saying, "I will swear on a stack of Bibles." Jesus taught our word should be so pure we never have to rely on some outward backing to assure its veracity.

He pointed out the silliness they invoked with their oaths. They started out big. They would swear by Heaven. That meant little in the day-to-day life of the average Israelite, so they lowered their sights a bit and used the earth as backing for their oath. Since both belong to God, what part could be used to back up a pledge? Knowing it carried little weight, they moved their attention to the Temple, which belonged to none of them. Then they lowered themselves to something more personal: the hair on their head. Jesus told them they could not make one hair on their head white or black.

Jesus was making a simple point. Don't live in a way you have to use oaths. Let your word be simple and straightforward. Live in such a way when people hear you say something, they know they can depend on you keeping your word.

I remember being taught it was wrong to put one's hand on a Bible and "swear to tell the truth, the whole truth, and nothing but the truth." Instead, we were to say, "I affirm." Did you know that's in the law books? It is there because a famous Quaker minister, George Fox, refused to swear on the Bible, so they put in him jail. He countered that the Bible they wanted to use for his swearing ceremony demanded he never lie. After his ordeal, a law was passed whereby a Christian could "affirm" instead of "swear."

I agree, that's splitting a semantical frog hair seven ways. I contend the command given here by Jesus is not about political oaths or legal matters. It is about everyday life. My life should be so good, so trustworthy, I should never have to do anything to make you believe I am telling the truth. So, if you find yourself testifying in a courtroom or taking the oath of the presidency of the United States, be sure to live such life when people hear you speak, they know they can depend upon your word.

> "You have heard that it was said, 'An eye for an eye and a tooth for a tooth.' But I tell you not to resist an evil person. But whoever slaps you on your right cheek, turn the other to him also. If anyone wants to sue you and take away your tunic, let him have your cloak also. And whoever compels you to go one mile, go with him two. Give to him who asks you, and from him who wants to borrow from you do not turn away.
>
> "You have heard that it was said, 'You shall love your neighbor and hate your enemy.' But I say to you, love your enemies, bless those who curse you, do good to those who hate you, and pray for those who spitefully use you and persecute you, that you may be sons of your Father in heaven; for He makes His sun rise on the evil and on the good, and sends rain on the just and on the unjust. For if you love those who love you, what reward have you? Do not even the tax collectors do the same? And if you greet your brethren only, what do you do more than others? Do not even the tax collectors do so? Therefore you shall be perfect, just as your Father in heaven is perfect" (Matthew 5:38–48).

I have purposely lumped two of His "You have heard . . . but I say to you" statements together. Both can easily be researched and can stand alone, but I see a connection between the two. In both cases, someone is offended, hurt, or mistreated. In both cases, Jesus' response is the same: *Forgive anyone who does you wrong.* I don't know anything that gives us more trouble than this command nor anything that can release more of God's Spirit in our lives more than complying with this command.

It appears Jesus is telling us to stand still and take whatever anyone wishes to throw at us, and indeed some understand His words that way. Before you jump on board and become a total pacifist, think for a moment. Are you asserting Jesus insists that if you are walking down the street with your family, you are to stand still and watch while some thugs attack your loved ones? I do not think Moses nor Jesus intended us to come away believing this.

My reasoning comes from taking these words and laying them alongside other passages in Scripture. For instance, why would the Holy Spirit, who inspired and filled the Son of God, have Paul write this: *"You therefore must endure hardship as a good soldier of Jesus Christ. No one engaged in warfare entangles himself with the affairs of this life, that he may please him who enlisted him as a soldier"* (2 Timothy 2:3-4)?

There is no way the Holy Spirit would use the idea of being a "good soldier" of Jesus if it were antithetical to living for Christ. Likewise, when Roman soldiers asked John the Baptist—a man Jesus called the "greatest born among women" (Luke 7:28)—what they had to do to flee from the wrath to come, John didn't tell them to turn in their commission and abandon their calling because it sometimes required violence on their part. Instead, John told the soldiers to be content with their pay, never use force to intimidate others, and never falsely accuse anyone (Luke 3:14). If they had to leave the military to follow Jesus, John would have been explicit in his demands. Since none were included, we must weigh the statements recorded by Matthew alongside other passages in Scripture.

How, then, are we to take the words of Jesus? How are we to apply these teachings to our lives? I think it all flows back to the opening Beatitudes. Remember, the rabbis of Jesus' day would give a short statement, then enlarge on it as time progressed. I think Jesus was harkening back to one of His earlier statements: *"Blessed are those who are persecuted for righteousness' sake, for theirs is the kingdom of heaven. Blessed are you when they revile and persecute you, and say all kinds of evil against you falsely for my name's sake. Rejoice and be exceedingly glad, for great is your reward in heaven, for so they persecuted the prophets who were before you" (Matthew 5:10-12).*

Jesus was saying we should not fight back when evil arises against us *because of the Gospel.* When we are attacked because of our stand for Jesus, we should not lash out, strike people with physical blows, or blow them up. It does little good to say we stand for the Prince of Peace and then use violence to back up our claim.

In fact, Jesus offers a counter-cultural idea about our enemies. Instead of assaulting them, He calls on us to take them before the Father in prayer. Imagine the paradox of this command. You and I are attacked because we love Jesus, and Jesus demands we stand strong and pray for them (Matthew 5:44)! I don't want to forgive and pray for them; I want to fight them and stand up for my rights. Jesus says, "Nope, you cannot act that way. Instead, love them, bless them, do good to them, and pray for them." That is a Kingdom ethic we hear little teaching about but must grasp to be effective witnesses.

Simply getting along with people is not enough. Jesus calls for the ongoing display of good works toward others. He demands generosity.

> "Take heed that you do not do your charitable deeds before men, to be seen by them. Otherwise you have no reward from your Father in heaven. Therefore, when you do a charitable deed, do not

> sound a trumpet before you as the hypocrites do in the synagogues and in the streets, that they may have glory from men. Assuredly, I say to you, they have their reward. But when you do a charitable deed, do not let your left hand know what your right hand is doing, that your charitable deed may be in secret; and your Father who sees in secret will Himself reward you openly" (Matthew 6:1-4).

As believers, we should be givers. There is something about the nature of a born-again person that wants to give. If we are not motivated to help others, we should spend time alone with the Master and let Him speak to our hearts. After all, Jesus did not say "if" you give, but "when" you give. He calls on us to be generous people.

However, we should act secretly and allow Him to reward us. You and I should strive to do our charitable work so no one knows we are the source from which it came. In my years in ministry, I have met many who would give if their attached strings were utilized. One man said he would give if he could see his name somewhere because of his gift. How unlike the Kingdom heart our Master requires!

Tough sledding, isn't it? Jesus calls on us to be totally different people. He demands we become more than simply "better sinners"; His ultimatum is for us to become "perfect" as our Father is perfect. That's because He is not interested in patching up a broken world, He wants to revolutionize it. He wants to fill the earth with His glory through our lives, lived out daily in the face of every adversity that comes our way. May He find us faithful!

SERMON OUTLINE

Introduction: These words deserve a lifetime of study and application. Perhaps the time has come for the local church (indeed every believer) to once more dive deep into the teachings of Jesus contained here and do more than seek to search for hidden nuances. Maybe, just maybe, it is time for us to take seriously these teachings and consider them pillars of His Kingdom, if not requirements for discipleship. The Master is telling us what it means to be in His kingdom.

1. PREPARING FOR THE FINAL EXAM
   a. Required Courses
   b. Research Into the Subject
   c. Remaining Close to the Teacher
2. PRACTICES OF THE CHRISTIAN LIFE
   a. Preserving Like Salt
   b. Penetrating Like Light
   c. Practical Application of the Truth
3. PATTERNS OF CHRISTIAN BEHAVIOR
   a. Murder
   b. Marriage: Adultery and Divorce
   c. Mankind: Truth-Telling, Forgiveness, and Generosity

Conclusion: This is some tough sledding. Jesus demands we become totally different people in a world that resists change. He calls for this because He is uninterested in making us better sinners. His ultimatum is for you and me to become perfect, even as His Father is perfect. He is not interested in patching up our broken world. His goal is to revolutionize it through His glory revealed in our lives. May He find us faithful in seeking to be His vessels.

STUDY QUESTIONS

1. What do you think Jesus meant when He declared our righteousness must be greater than the Scribes and Pharisees? How does that play out in our day?
2. How can we be salt and light in our culture?
3. What does the fulfillment of the Law and Prophets by Jesus mean to us? What does this imply about our daily conduct?
4. How do you feel about the author's treatment of murder? Is it possible for one to serve in a position in our society that requires the occasional use of violence and be a Christian? Why do you think as you do?
5. Divorce. Share your thoughts on this heart-breaking subject. How do your thoughts align with those expressed by Jesus?
6. Discuss how our culture disguises untruths and truth? How is this affecting our lives?
7. How can you adopt these teachings into your everyday life?

3

THE GREATEST SERMON EVER, PART III

> "Enter by the narrow gate; for wide is the gate and broad is the way that leads to destruction, and there are many who go in by it. Because narrow is the gate and difficult is the way which leads to life, and there are few who find it" (Matthew 7:13-14).

After focusing on our relationships with others, Jesus drills into how to better our walk with God. We will discover the power to enact the ethics of the Kingdom previously laid out before us.

We must be careful about avoiding extremes. Some of us get so caught up in relationships with other people that we forget the need to stay plugged into God. Others of us, especially Pentecostals and Charismatics, can focus so much on staying in touch with God that we forget He has called on us to get along with each other on the journey.

Jesus wants us to let our light shine, showing Him the only source of brightness. He wants us to be salty believers, living so as to make others thirsty for Him. Yet, the only way we can maintain any saltiness is through developing a constant, ongoing relationship with Him.

Importance of Relationship

Matthew introduced the idea that some will not discover the way into the Kingdom. Luke, in his retelling of this sermon, condensed and phrased it a bit differently. I have no doubt Jesus taught this more than once, so Luke might have been referencing a totally different occasion, but here is his rendering: "*Strive to enter through the narrow gate, for many, I say to you, will seek to enter and will not be able*" (13:24).

Jesus said you and I must "strive" to enter the gate. *Strive* means to struggle for a prize, to contend with an adversary, to endeavor to do something difficult with great zeal. In that era, this word meant being an athlete who worked feverishly in the gym to win a medal. Also, it described the fury with which a soldier went into battle, determined to destroy the enemy and win the war,

Does that sound contrary to the "easy believe-ism" permeating churches today? Yes! In our day, all someone needs to do is sign a card, mutter a repeated prayer, get wet in the right pool, or try any of the other ways we "count noses" in the church. I believe Jesus would be turned off by the ease with which we think we enter the Kingdom. After all, He told us to devote our energy, passion, and time to ensuring our entrance into the gate.

It would probably startle some of us if Jesus spoke today. He might have the nerve to tell us we must put as much passion into going after Him as we do in seeking money. He might tell some of us that passion for entertainment and sports should instead be applied to ensuring we make it in. He might shock us by saying our career, our kids countless activites, and all the stuff that consumes the modern lifestyle should not be the uppermost concern. Instead, we must passionately chase after eternal things.

No, this is not "works salvation." That price has already been paid; the gateway has already been opened. Our struggle is getting to and through that gate. If you doubt what I am saying, pay close attention to two words Jesus used.

First, He talked about something "narrow." This implies a small opening between great obstacles. It is like trying to wedge between a couple of narrow pews in a church. You might have to set a few things aside to make it to your seat. You might have to twist a bit, making an uncomfortable adjustment, to make it into the pew. That's what Jesus is trying to get across to us. If we really want to enter this gate, we will have to drop some things that hold us back. Why, we might even have to get into a kneeling position in order to make it through this narrow entrance!

Not everyone who hangs around the coffee bar in a church foyer will walk through the pearly gates. That's strong and judgmental, but I am only parroting what Scripture has been telling us all along:

- *"'The wolf and the lamb shall feed together. The lion shall eat straw like the ox, and dust shall be the serpent's food. They shall not hurt nor destroy in all My holy mountain,' says the Lord"* (Isaiah 65:25).
- *"Do you not know that the unrighteous will not inherit the kingdom of God? Do not be deceived. Neither fornicators, nor idolaters, nor adulterers, nor homosexuals, nor sodomites" (*1 Corinthians 6:9).
- *"But the cowardly, unbelieving, abominable, murderers, sexually immoral, sorcerers, idolaters, and all liars shall have their part in the lake which burns with fire and brimstone, which is the second death" (Revelation 21:8).*

Some patterns of behavior will not be part of that celestial city. Regardless of what it takes, no matter how hard we try to conform our lives to the ethical demands made by Christ Jesus, it is a narrow way.

The second term intensifies the matter: Jesus used the word *difficult.* Once we have found the gate, we are only at the beginning. Even after we decide to enter, we will face some difficult decisions. For instance, we have to face the difficult choice of setting aside the time required to walk with the Lord. And what about those things that hinder our relationship with God? Are we going to lay them aside, even though it is extremely hard and painful to do so? While walking with Jesus is easy in some seasons, are we willing to wade through those difficult seasons?

Importance of Remaining Before God

Lest you think me too stringent, read closely once more the haunting refrain of Jesus: *"Enter by the narrow gate; for wide is the gate and broad is the way that leads to destruction, and there are many who go in by it, because narrow is the gate and difficult is the way which leads to life, and there are few who find it"* (Matthew 7:13-14).

We select one of those roads every day. We make decisions, sometimes hard decisions, about staying on the path. I do not believe any of us deliberately chooses the road to destruction. I have never met anyone who wanted to become an alcoholic or drug addict. Nor do I know any woman who woke up one morning with the intention of becoming pregnant so she could later have her baby ripped apart by a partial-birth abortion. No one among us thinks, *I want to destroy my family!*

Of course, the answer to all the above is a resounding "No!" If that is the case, we must decide to do whatever it takes to follow Jesus. We must move with great deliberation toward a life dominated by the struggle to enter and walk the narrow way. Thankfully, Jesus outlines how to remain in close contact with the Father.

In this great sermon, Jesus addressed five areas of our lives that deal with our relationship with God. Three of them are actions—observable things that make a statement not only to God but to all who observe our lives. Two are attitudes—inner qualities from which the three actions spring. The striving mentioned above deals with these five areas. If we pursue these five areas of walking with God, we will one day hear a hearty "Well done!" from the Master.

Jesus on Prayer

> "And when you pray, you shall not be like the hypocrites, for they love to pray standing in the synagogues and on the corners of the streets, that they may be seen by men. Assuredly, I say to you, they have their reward. But you, when you pray, go into your room, and when you have shut your door, pray to your Father who is in the secret place; and your Father who sees in secret will reward you openly. And when you pray, do not use vain repetitions as the heathen do, for they think that they will be heard for their many words.
>
> Therefore do not be like them, for your Father knows the things you have need of before you ask Him. In this manner, therefore, pray: Our Father in heaven, Hallowed be Your name. Your kingdom come, Your will be done on earth as it is in heaven. Give us this day our daily bread, and forgive us our debts, as we forgive our debtors. And do not lead us into temptation, but deliver us from the evil one.

> For Yours is the kingdom and the power and the glory forever. Amen" (Matthew 6:5–13).
>
> "Ask, and it will be given to you; seek, and you will find; knock, and it will be opened to you. For everyone who asks receives, and he who seeks finds, and to him who knocks it will be opened. Or what man is there among you who, if his son asks for bread, will give him a stone? Or if he asks for a fish, will he give him a serpent? If you then, being evil, know how to give good gifts to your children, how much more will your Father who is in heaven give good things to those who ask Him!" (7:7-11).

In these two separate teachings, Jesus demonstrates the vast vista of prayer that opens before His children: If we are going to walk with God, prayer is a must. It is that simple.

Prayer is to be practiced. Jesus never said, "If you pray." He always couched His teaching on the assumption that children of Heaven pray.

Prayer is to be personal. Jesus excoriated the religious leaders of His day because their prayers were public, done so they would be considered righteous by those who heard them. It is not that Jesus was against public praying; He did some Himself. Nor is Jesus teaching against praying repeatedly for an answer. In fact, that is the opposite of what He tells us in Matthew 7. Jesus is driving at personal, self-emptying prayer.

Our prayers must be personal because of the call for surrender. We are taught it is not our will, plans, and desires. Rather, real prayer is about surrendering our will to Him. Our prayers must be personal because of the call for repentance. Jesus taught us to ask for forgiveness, and His response is attached to our forgiving others. He taught us to spend some time in prayer about our weak areas and how He can help us to defeat the evil one. If there is an area where prayer really gets personal, it is here. We all struggle with specific areas of frailty and have the ever-pressing need to get alone with Him and overcome our weaknesses. Our prayers must also be personal simply because of life's stuff. We must pray about all the junk, the daily routine, and the mundane things we all struggle with. We are instructed to pray about things we encounter daily.

What a God we serve! Far from being detached and aloof in Heaven, our God is deeply interested in our daily affairs. He longs to be invited into the arena of our existence. Nothing, no matter how trivial it may appear to us, is so small it escapes His peering concern. I am thrilled that nothing, no matter how huge and intimidating, is so massive it stunts His ability to work His glorious plan in my life! I think that was the end Paul was driving at when he wrote, *"Don't worry about anything; instead, pray about everything. Tell God what you need and thank Him for all He has done"* (Philippians 4:6 NLT).

One final thought about prayer: It has to be perennial. I believe we are taught this by one word Jesus used in Matthew 7. We are told to ask for *daily* bread. If we are to pray on a daily basis for the necessities of life, which bread represents, we must also involve ourselves in a never-ending cycle of prayer for everything else.

You and I will never be able to live out what He has taught us without divine intervention. We will never summon from within the strength needed to be what He has called us to be. We must have His enablement, which starts with our contacting God through prayer. To make the difficult choices required of us, we will forever be placed in a position of prayerful requests for His help. We don't have to make an ostentatious display of this prayer. In fact, we don't have to let anyone know we are in need. All that is required for a meeting with God is to draw away into that private place where we meet with Him for fellowship (Matthew 6:6).

Jesus On Fasting

> "Moreover, when you fast, do not be like the hypocrites, with a sad countenance. For they disfigure their faces that they may appear to men to be fasting. Assuredly, I say to you, they have their reward. But you, when you fast, anoint your head and wash your face, so that you do not appear to men to be fasting, but to your Father who is in the secret place; and your Father who sees in secret will reward you openly" (Matthew 6:16–18).

I have books in my library that propose fasting as the cure-all for every ill in society. They promise vast power with God. They regale the reader with notices that if done according to their plan, fasting will result in fantastic encounters with the supernatural. If, according to these authors, you fast long and often enough like they do, the same things will happen in your life that have transpired in theirs. My problem with their awesome claims lies in the personal nature of fasting, as described by Jesus.

In the same manner as He did when addressing prayer, Jesus did not say "if" but "when." Fasting is a given in the Kingdom. He then proceeded to teach us a bit about proper fasting, but He did not make this a major point of teaching. He did, however, let us know we must not develop wrong ideas about fasting. For instance, much of the modern teaching regarding fasting implies that our fasting changes God. It somehow bends Him to our will. That borders on blasphemy. Fasting does not change

God; it changes me. The same goes for all the other actions in the faith. My praying doesn't change God; it changes me. My church attendance does not change God; it changes me. My giving does not change God; it changes me.

Simply put, *fasting* is going without food to draw closer to God. Throughout Scripture, men and women fasted as a means of seeking God's plan and bending themselves to His will. In the early church, believers fasted and prayed as they conducted church business (Acts 13:2-3). When they sought to humble themselves before the Lord, they fasted (Ezra 8:21). When suffering defeat and seeking the Lord for victory, His people fasted (Judges 20:26). God's people, in times of repentance and seeking God for safety in judgment, were told to engage in fasting (Joel 2:12-13). Fasting is a means of clearing our hearts and minds so we can discern God's will (Daniel 9:3).

Isaiah 58:6-7 gives us a definitive message about fasting: *"Is this not the fast that I have chosen: to loose the bonds of wickedness, to undo the heavy burdens, to let the oppressed go free, and that you break every yoke? Is it not to share your bread with the hungry, and that you bring to your house the poor who are cast out; when you see the naked, that you cover him, and not hide yourself from your own flesh?"*

God looks for the fast that humbles and places us in a position to minister to others. Proper fasting enables ordinary people to become extraordinary servants of the Lord. That's why Jesus calls us to fast. When questioned why He and his disciples were not fasting, Jesus said times of fasting would be part of the disciple's lives after He was gone (Matthew 9:14-15).

That being said, how should those of us who are not experienced in this discipline initiate fasting into our lives? How do we go about it?

First, if you have never fasted before, don't try to take on a forty-day fast as recorded in Scripture. You will either kill yourself or break your fast, and the enemy will pile guilt all over you. Also, if you have health problems and cannot go without food (not the glandular problem with which I struggle: I have a mouth that loves to eat!), find another way to deny yourself before the Lord. Start small and learn how to bend yourself before Him.

Second, do not fall into a religious trap. Just because someone else fasts a certain period does not mean you must do the same. Find your own pace, discover what works for you, and grow in your walk with Jesus.

Third, don't think that because you go without food, you are fasting. We often joke about missing a meal because of time restraints. We kiddingly say, "Oh well, I will just call it a fast and get credit for it." Missing some intake of food for reasons other than those stated in Scripture has another name: dieting. Fasting involves slowing down and allowing God to break into your life, not skipping a meal because the schedule was so hectic you didn't have time to eat.

Fourth, don't brag about fasting. You don't have to tell anyone you are fasting to receive their adulation. In fact, when you do that, you've already broken the reason why you should be fasting. However, just a word of caution here: If you plan to fast, let your spouse know before they prepare a meal.

Fifth, just do it! Start small and discover the joy that comes with the sense of Christ's presence that will fill your heart.

Any study of a revival or breakthrough from Heaven will reveal an individual or a group immersing themselves in fasting and prayer. These two elements of obedience, linked together, will open our hearts and lives to a fresh infusion of His presence and power. We all know we need more power from on high.

We are all painfully aware of our deficiency in advancing His Kingdom. Once we discover the power involved in linking fasting and prayer, even the most difficult of situations will bow to His authority (Matthew 17:21).

Jesus on Giving

> "Do not lay up for yourselves treasures on earth, where moth and rust destroy and where thieves break in and steal; but lay up for yourselves treasures in heaven, where neither moth nor rust destroys and where thieves do not break in and steal. For where your treasure is, there your heart will be also" (Matthew 6:19–21).

The issue here is generosity of heart. Jesus warns us against a spirit of hoarding, where we find security in the accumulation of stuff. His message is clear and succinct: Either we own our stuff, or it will own us! His words are cutting and sober: We cannot serve God and money! The sobering truth is if we cannot give away money or possessions, they will own us rather than us owning them.

You have probably never heard of Bertha Adams, who lived alone in Florida. When she died at age 71, everyone thought of her as a pitiful woman who barely survived. She lived in a trash-filled apartment. She constantly begged for food from her neighbors, and all her clothes came from the Salvation Army. From all appearances, she was a penniless person who barely survived.

After her death, it was discovered Bertha had not one but two safe deposit boxes in different banks. When the stocks, bonds, and cash were totaled, she had died a millionaire.[1]

---

[1] Kent Hughes, *The Sermon on the Mount* (Wheaton, IL: Crossway, 2001), 205.

This happened because Bertha's stuff owned her. It told her to pinch, scrap, hoard, and do all she could to accumulate more. Any life driven by stuff cannot walk in agreement with God.

Jesus attacked His listeners' sources of security. He leveled accusations at three areas of life that comprised their sense of well-being. He let them know their clothing was not a source of security. Like our day, expensive clothing is a sign saying to others, "I am doing well!" Of course, they had moths in their day, as do we. To complicate matters, they did not have the moth repellants we have at our disposal. So, they fully understood the aggravation of going to collect a favorite garment, only to discover it had been destroyed by moths.

Jesus equally attacked their sense of security found in food. When Jesus used the word *rust,* He was talking about something being eaten away; He was not referencing a rusting car. He was talking about rats or other vermin eating away their stored food. Jesus reminded them that regardless of the grain they stored up, worms and rats would grow fat on their labor and devour their security.

Jesus then moved to their most prized possession—money. They would bury valuables in their homes, sometimes in the walls, but a thief could dig just as they could.

In one church I was pastoring years ago, some thieves decided they wanted to break into our gym. I have no idea why; there was absolutely nothing of value in that old, rusty building. I guess they didn't know that, for they worked hard on getting in. How? They took off the door frame and then unfastened the metal siding. They invested a lot of work, removing dozens of screws. Why they stopped, I don't know. My guess is they decided it was too much work. They had no idea they were enacting something Jesus warned us about. No matter where we place our valuables, there are dedicated thieves who can work hard to steal them. We cannot trust the things that can be easily taken from us.

Before we decide Jesus is against saving money, stop and take a breath. In fact, the opposite is true. The Book of Proverbs tells us to prepare for the future. Jesus is forbidding an attitude and actions that state, "I am going to get all I can, can all I can, and then go bury the can!" He is calling on us to be balanced in our attitudes and actions about the future.

A couple of common-sense statements based on Scripture can guide us. First, we need to remember *we will not take it with us.* I once heard of an old miser who lived engulfed in scrapping together every penny possible. He never enjoyed anything, and he discovered at the end that all his wealth could not buy one extra minute of life. Devoted to being a miser to the end, he called his doctor, attorney, and a pastor from a church he had never attended to his deathbed. Telling them how he had heard all his life, "You can't take it with you," he placed in the hand of each individual an envelope with fifty thousand dollars. He told them at his burial, they were to toss the envelopes into his casket. He was going to beat the system. He was going to take it with him.

The day of his funeral came, and each man dutifully walked up to the casket and tossed in the envelope they had been given. Later, at the funeral home, the attorney confessed, "I have to be honest. I am building a counseling center for those with legal needs, so I took out twenty thousand and tossed in thirty." The doctor spoke next and lamented, "I guess I must be honest. I am building a clinic for the poor and I kept out thirty grand and only threw in twenty." Looking smug and aloof, the minister said, "I am shocked that you, leading citizens of our city, would sink to such a low degree. I threw in a personal check for the entire fifty grand!"

Second, 1 Timothy 6:17-19 says, *"Command those who are rich in this present age not to be haughty, nor to trust in uncertain riches but in the living God, who gives us richly all things to enjoy. Let them do good, that they be rich in good works, ready to give, willing to share, storing up for themselves a good foundation for the time to come, that they may lay hold on eternal life."*

You may be thinking, "That lets me off the hook! I am not rich." Think again. Paul did not say, "Tell those who are rich according to twenty-first century North America." Most of us are unfamiliar with his worldview, which places most of us in the category of "rich." If you have a few dollars lying around your house, you have more money than most of the world's population.

This is not about having abundant money; it's about letting some money have you. God calls us to give liberally in support of His work. Not because He needs the money but because this is the antidote to the tyranny of a few dollars driving us to spiritual bankruptcy. By giving to God, you are storing up riches in Heaven. When you invest in missions, you send things ahead to the other side. When you give to the poor, you are investing in your eternal home.

Importance of Relying on God

Moving from actions called for in the life of the believer, Jesus shifts to two important attitudes which are important, for they are the soil from which the right actions spring. The first, fear, is a crippling attitude that manifests in many areas of our lives. In fact, fear can immobilize a saint to the point of disbelief.

Jesus on Fear

> "Therefore I say to you, do not worry about your life, what you will eat or what you will drink; nor about your body, what you will put on. Is not life more than food and the body more than clothing? Look at the birds of the air, for they neither sow nor reap nor gather into barns; yet your heavenly Father feeds them. Are you not of more value than they? Which of you by worrying can add one cubit to his stature? So why do you worry about clothing? Consider the lilies of the field, how they grow: they neither toil nor spin; and yet I say to you that even Solomon in all his glory was not arrayed like one of these. Now if God so clothes the grass of the field, which today is, and tomorrow is thrown into the oven, will He not much more clothe you, O you of little faith?
>
> Therefore do not worry, saying, 'What shall we eat?' or 'What shall we drink?' or 'What shall we wear?' For after all these things the Gentiles seek. For your heavenly Father knows that you need all these things. But seek first the kingdom of God and His righteousness, and all these things shall be added to you. Therefore do not worry about tomorrow, for tomorrow will worry about its own things. Sufficient for the day is its own trouble" (Matthew 6:25–34).

Three times in this passage, we are told, "Do not worry." The Greek word translated as *worry* means "to have a divided mind." Our English word comes from an old German word that means "to strangle." Jesus does not want us to be divided, torn apart, and have the joy of life choked out of us over things we cannot control.

This is not a devil-may-care attitude. We are taught to number our days, to strive for excellence, to prepare for the future, and to do our best. Jesus is not excusing us from the routines that require our concentration and effort. This is not an excuse to be lazy, to just let happen what will happen. Instead, Jesus informs us not to be torn apart over things we cannot control. We should not allow the fear of things that may or may not happen to shove us into the abyss of unbelief in God.

How did Jesus illustrate this attitude? He pointed to the birds and flowers. They are cared for and provided for by the Father, who assures us we are worth much more than them. Perhaps Jesus pointed to a short guy and said if worrying could make him taller, this guy would be a power forward in the NBA. Not really, but he confirmed that worrying about height does not enable one to grow taller. Likewise, fretting over losing hair does not empower one to grow new follicles. If that worked, many of us would still have a lustrous mop of real hair on our balding scalps! None of us can sit around and worry about death and add time to our lifespan, so why obsess about it? Jesus said we should trust God and move on.

Jesus calls on us to employ two tactics to defeat fear. First, we must put Him at the head of the line in our lives. Seek Him and His ways, trust what He said is true, and He will take care of us. Second, do the first thing every day. Living in such a fashion will banish fear from our lives.

Jesus on Judging Others

We have reached the final segment of His teaching about our attitudes. He nails us about being critical, overbearing, judgmental people.

> "Judge not, that you be not judged. For with what judgment you judge, you will be judged; and with the measure you use, it will be measured back to you. And why do you look at the speck in your brother's eye, but do not consider the plank in your own eye? Or how can you say to your brother, 'Let me remove the speck from your eye'; and look, a plank is in your own eye? Hypocrite! First remove the plank from your own eye, and then you will see clearly to remove the speck from your brother's eye. Do not give what is holy to the dogs; nor cast your pearls before swine, lest they trample them under their feet, and turn and tear you in pieces" (Matthew 7:1–6).

Some of us need this message more than any other Jesus delivered. We can come to the place where we think that because we do not have the glaring problems that plague others, we are above being judged. Sadly, the longer some of us hang around the church, the greater our tendency to look upon others with disdain and judgment.

Jesus referenced a critical spirit that is aware of everyone's faults but their own. We fall into this trap when we spend time hunting for specks of sawdust others have while we are walking around with huge planks protruding from our eyes. When we estimate we are always right and everyone else is wrong, we miss the blind spots in our lives and are prone to using our abundant planks to beat up on anyone who dares question our excellent vision!

There's the story of a young man who kept bringing prospective brides home to meet his parents. No matter their appearance and how nice they were, Mom never approved. The young man's friend suggested he bring home a woman who was as much like his mother as possible. Finally, he happened to find the right girl. After a few dates, he took her home to meet his parents. His mom loved her. This young lady enjoyed the same things, liked the same food, and laughed at the same things as his mom. There was only one problem—his dad hated her!

Here's how to tell when a hyper-critical spirit is rising. When I am critical, my language betrays me. When speaking of my issues, I use euphemisms to soften the blow, but when speaking about someone else's shortcomings, I employ harsh terms. For example, my lack of truthfulness is due to tact or a need-to-know basis, but the other person is a liar! My greed is disguised as watching out for tomorrow and being sure my family is taken care of. The other person is a stingy miser. I am attracted to the opposite sex, but the other person is filled with lust. I need to rest on Sunday, so I stay home and miss church. The other person doesn't love Jesus enough to get out of bed. I believe in the truth and don't mind speaking my mind. The other person, however, is embittered and mean-spirited. Get the idea?

Jesus was clear here, so you and I must sit up and pay close attention. If I judge you too harshly, I will be judged by that same criterion. You and I will face our own system of evaluation one day! The next time you think you need to "lower the hammer" on someone for what they said or did, remember we should not slap the cuffs on them and drag them away. Instead, we are urged to display mercy just like we want God to show us (Luke 6:36).

If I want God to be merciful and longsuffering with me, I must display that toward others. I must be merciful and gracious.

Do you realize what happens when someone plagued by guilt staggers into one of our gatherings and discovers grace and mercy? Do you know what happens when they hear "forgiven" rather than "forsaken"? Do you have the slightest inclination toward the stupendous emotion in the life of the shame-ridden when they come around us, and instead of condemnation, they receive consolation? Can you imagine what will happen when the unreached community around your church learns they are wanted there instead of Christians wishing "bad folks" like them would leave? It sets people free. It tears down the devil's ability to build walls. It leads people to Christ, who can and will change their lives as they fall before Him. Oh, that we could be such houses of freedom!

As in all things, there are those among us who go too far and condemn all who are careful and exhibit discernment about people. Funny isn't it, how people who blast those who are balanced for being judgmental are themselves judgmental?

An issue in the modern church, especially in America, is that if we try to examine anyone at all, we are branded as critical, heresy hunters, fanatics, harsh, and Pharisaical. However, in this same sermon that condemns judgment, Jesus challenges us to be discriminating in our acceptance of others:

> "Beware of false prophets, who come to you in sheep's clothing, but inwardly they are ravenous wolves. You will know them by their fruits. Do men gather grapes from thornbushes or figs from thistles? Even so, every good tree bears good fruit, but a bad tree bears bad fruit. A good tree cannot bear bad fruit, nor can a bad tree bear good fruit. Every tree that does not bear good fruit is cut down and thrown into the fire. Therefore by their fruits you will know them" (Matthew 7:15–20).

Jesus plainly tells us to be particular about those we follow. We must be cautious about those we trust. On the one hand, we must be careful about judging people. On the other hand, we must be careful about who we entrust with our lives. This really is not hard to balance. I must cut you as much slack as I want and need God to grant me. I must be willing to work with your shortcomings just as I want God to work with mine. I need to be as merciful toward you as I want God to be toward me. But when it comes to following your leadership, I need to watch your life to make sure you are headed in the right direction. I need to be sure you know what you are talking about. I need to see your life becoming more like that of Jesus, and less like the culture around you.

Years back, Dr. Cecil B. Knight, former general overseer of the Church of God, spoke for me in a morning service. At the end of his message, he made a statement that seemed to come out of the blue. It had nothing to do with his sermon or the seeming moment. He said, "The church has a glaring absence of the gift of discernment," and it burned deep into my spirit. He was right. In our clamoring for gifts and blessings, we have overlooked this one. In our desire to be liked by everyone and accepted in the larger circles of the religious world, we have cast discernment aside. We have done so to our own detriment.

Years after Jesus gave us this warning, Paul said, *"Recognize those who labor among you, and are over you in the Lord and admonish you"* (1 Thessalonians 5:12).

The word *recognize* means "to gaze on someone, to watch them thoroughly." Recognizing someone is more than recalling their name; it is knowing them. It's being aware of what makes them tick, who they are, and what they really think.

We are not being judgmental when we watch someone's life to see if they live up to Scriptural norms. We are not being judgmental when we lay someone else's teaching down against the

Word of the Lord. It is not wrong to be cautious and to examine people and their teaching. In our day of no set standards, it is more important than ever. Oh, here's a hint: If someone starts to fight against scrutiny, you probably need to move on from them.

Quite a boatload of information, isn't it? Jesus has a lot to say about the way we think and act. Now, we must determine if we will take His preaching seriously or shrug our shoulders like His teachings are nothing more than an infomercial that we can watch and ignore. As we will see, our decision in this area can produce glorious or disastrous results.

SERMON OUTLINE

Introduction: Jesus spoke a lot about our relationships with each other. He gave us parameters in which we must live. He challenged us to live with such distinction that the world around us would wonder how ordinary people could live such extraordinary lives. They might not join us, but they will be amazed at the community of believers. Shifting His focus, Jesus then dove into the relationship we can have with God that will witness to our world.

1. IMPORTANCE OF RELATIONSHIP WITH THE FATHER
   a. Striving to Enter the Gate
   b. Startled to Discover the Truth
   c. Separation Required
2. IMPORTANCE OF REMAINING WITH THE FATHER
   a. Jesus on Prayer
   b. Jesus on Fasting
   c. Jesus on Giving
3. IMPORTANCE OF RELYING ON THE FATHER
   a. Jesus on Fear
   b. Jesus on Judging Others
   c. Jesus on Balance

Conclusion: The Master presents us with a vast amount of challenging material. His call for radical life change can revolutionize the church as we know it. Now, the decision falls on us to determine whether or not we take His teachings seriously or ignore them like an infomercial on television. Our decisions in this area can produce either glorious or disastrous outcomes.

STUDY QUESTIONS

1. When Jesus speaks of a "narrow gate," what comes to mind? What implications do His words carry today?
2. When speaking of "staying with the Father," how do the teachings of Jesus impact your life? Is your walk with the heavenly Father a daily exercise?
3. Jesus spoke about and modeled prayer. How important is prayer to your life? What practices of prayer are effective in your walk with God?
4. Have you ever fasted? If not, how might you begin practicing this discipline?
5. How is giving a vital part of your Christian lifestyle? Are you giving to God? To others?
6. What fears confront you? Do you regularly contend with worry? How does Jesus teach us to counter fear and worry?
7. Do you need God's forgiveness in your life? Do you grant others that same compassion? What is the relationship between us forgiving others and God forgiving us?

4

THE GREATEST SERMON EVER, PART IV

> "Therefore whoever hears these sayings of Mine, and does them, I will liken him to a wise man who built his house on the rock: and the rain descended, the floods came, and the winds blew and beat on that house; and it did not fall, for it was founded on the rock. But everyone who hears these sayings of Mine, and does not do them, will be like a foolish man who built his house on the sand: and the rain descended, the floods came, and the winds blew and beat on that house; and it fell. And great was its fall."
>
> And so it was, when Jesus had ended these sayings, that the people were astonished at His teaching, for He taught them as one having authority, and not as the scribes (Matthew 7:24–29).

Every great sermon has a rousing conclusion that grabs your attention and drives home the truth. The greatest sermon ever preached is no exception. As Jesus completed His copious teachings, it is easy to imagine the nice church attendees closing their Bibles, putting away their notepads and pens, getting ready to leave the church, and heading to Pizza Hut. Then, out of nowhere, Jesus added a stunning "oh-by-the-way" comment.

This teaching constitutes one of the most frightening sections in Scripture. Using a story to drive home His point, Jesus illustrated the danger we face in our walk with Him. His story was real and vital, and they had witnessed what Jesus referenced.

Everyone loves a good story, and one example is the story of a man named Frank who had a beautiful Labrador. This well-behaved dog never presented any problems.

One morning Frank looked out his window and saw his wonderful Lab with something dangling from both sides of his mouth. He was mortified when he realized it was a pet rabbit from a next-door neighbor. Wondering what to do, he took the dead rabbit from the dog's mouth, carried it inside and carefully bathed it, dried it with a blow dryer, and fluffed out the fur to make it look as good as possible. That night, under the cover of darkness, he slipped across the fence into his neighbor's yard and carefully put the rabbit into its cage.

The following day, the next-door neighbor banged on Frank's door. He was steaming mad. Frank went to the door, and his heart sank. There stood his neighbor, dead rabbit in hand. Before he could speak, his neighbor blurted out, "Frank, this is horrible! Sick! Our rabbit died three days ago, and I buried him in our yard. Now someone has dug him up, cleaned him up, and put him back in the cage. It's sick!"[1]

You may remember nothing from this chapter except the picture of a Lab with a dead rabbit in its mouth and Frank's feverish attempts to cover things up. When you think about that humorous image, remember the story's setting. Jesus was explaining that things are not always as they appear to be. Sometimes, things are at work under the surface.

---

[1] Charles Swindoll, *Simple Faith* (Nashville: Thomas Nelson, 1991), 243.

Jesus pointed out two homes under construction as an illustration to close out His sermon. There were two different builders and two opposite outcomes. Jesus frequently used a contrast of pairs in His sermons. He spoke of two groups of people preparing for a wedding (Matthew 22:1-14). One group made the necessary adjustments, one did not. He taught us there are two roads in life—one leading to Heaven, the other to hell (7:13-14). He said two men will be working in the field (24:40) and two women grinding at a mill when He suddenly returns (v. 41). In each case, one will depart, and the other will remain.

There is no convoluted thinking with Jesus that tries to blur everything in life. He draws a line and says, "Pick one side or the other. Be careful what you choose." He does this again by telling us about two builders—two ways of constructing our lives. This summation is vital.

The building project was not a momentary event. So many of us have bought into the false idea that all we must do is have some moment, some crisis event with the Master, and then we are free to pursue our own interests and neglect anything spiritual. This story says the notion that we can "accept" Jesus as our Savior and then do nothing more is a fallacy. Coming to Jesus is not the end; it is only the beginning.

Anyone who has built a house understands Jesus' teaching. Sometimes, we understand it painfully. Here's a rule of thumb on building a house or a church facility: It will take longer than they say and cost more than expected! That said, we won't be "super saints" two weeks after accepting Christ. Conversely, we shouldn't be the same twenty years from now. No one is willing to work on a house year after year without seeing progress toward completion. Jesus wants us to grow up and become established and profitable buildings, which will bring Him glory.

Every one of us is building a life. Be it good or bad, we are building. The outstanding Methodist minister Clovis Chappel (1882-1972) said:

> We are building all the time, whether wisely or foolishly. We are building by everything we do. We are building by every thought we think. We are building by every word we speak, every dream we dream, every ambition we cherish. All these go to make up the material that enters into the structure that we are building for the ages.
>
> Some of us are putting shoddy stuff into our buildings. We are putting material that cannot stand the test of the storm. The oath that you swore, that thoughtless blasphemy that you flung from your lips, that was poor material. The foul story that you told, that unclean thing that you did, that too was shoddy. That time you ran with the multitude to do evil out of sheer cowardice; that time when you remained silent when you should have spoken out. . . that, too, was poor stuff to put into your soul temple. That time you clutched your money in the midst of a pressing need; that time you passed by on the other side when a wounded life was calling for you. . . that also was shoddy. The fact that you are standing today, though a member of the church, with your membership hidden away in the country or buried in your trunk, trying to play neutral when God needs soldiers. . . that means you are putting flimsy stuff into your building.[2]

---

[2] Clovis Chappel, *Preaching on the Words of Jesus* (Grand Rapids: Baker, 1997), 218-19.

The need for quality and lasting effort becomes evident when we consider something beneath the surface of what Jesus taught. Everyone, including the righteous, has storms blowing into their lives. Years back, I had a medical doctor in Birmingham who would say, "Alas, Reverend, even the godly have germs." The time I went in with pneumonia, I heartily agreed. Like germs, the godly also have storms—often large and horrendous storms.

Both houses in the story of Jesus came under attack. Both houses were subjected to duress and stress. We need to be careful not to read too much into the presence of storms, or sunlight, for that matter. Both come to us regardless of how godly or spiritual we happen to be. Jesus was not teaching about a stormproof religion, an exemption from the ordinary trials of life. Instead, as He winds down this powerful sermon, He calls on us to build a spiritual house which, when built upon Him as a sure foundation, will withstand the inevitable attacks from life's storms.

This message of Jesus is not about being so powerful the storms fear you. Nor is it about being so godly the storms dare not come your way. Instead, this is about what is left standing when the storm has stripped away everything it can possibly steal. Jesus is all about building your house on such a great foundation that when all is said and done, you will rise from the wind and rain in victory.

Read again the chronicle of Job. He had lost everything and considered himself a dying man, and yet, the Spirit of God arose in Job as he said:

> "Oh, that my words were written! Oh, that they were inscribed in a book! That they were engraved on a rock with an iron pen and lead, forever!

> For I know that my Redeemer lives, and He shall stand at last on the earth; And after my skin is destroyed, this I know, that in my flesh I shall see God, Whom I shall see for myself, and my eyes shall behold, and not another. How my heart yearns within me!" (Job 19:23–27).

Dietrich Bonhoeffer embodied this victory. He was killed by the Nazis just days before the end of World War II. His crime? He preached Jesus, not the god of the German state, Adolph Hitler. On the final day of his life, he was convinced by his fellow prisoners to preach a sermon. He consented and began with, "By His stripes we are healed." While he was preaching, soldiers dragged him to the gallows and murdered him. They then took down his body and burned it. They also burned his briefcase and his manuscript. Did you catch that last part? Just a few hours from death in a hellish place, Bonhoeffer was studying and writing about Jesus.

That is genuine victory. Not the fluff most of us are addicted to. We are so consumed with the "stuff" of the American life that we miss how Jesus can lead us to a place where we are so strong in the power of His might that nothing—not even horrific persecution and murder by the state—can estrange us from His love.

Commentary by Paul

The Apostle Paul expounded on the sermon of Jesus in Ephesians 4:13-14: *"Till we all come to the unity of the faith and of the knowledge of the Son of God, to a perfect man, to the measure of the stature of the fullness of Christ; that we should no longer be children, tossed to and fro and carried about with every wind of doctrine, by the trickery of men, in the cunning craftiness of deceitful plotting."*

Paul tells us to grow up and become mature believers. We are to stop being children in the Lord and press on to stability and growth in the faith. Then Paul, like Jesus, warns us things will come our way that seek to destroy our walk with Christ. Jesus talked about destruction caused by rain. Paul spoke of floods of persecution and winds of false doctrine aroused by false teachers. The phrase *"the trickery of men"* in Greek is the root word from which we derive our English word *dice*. Allowing the teaching of the false prophets to infiltrate our lives, coupled with the pressure of persecution, is like getting into a crapshoot with the devil. I can tell you who will win that game. We are playing against one who always uses loaded dice!

I read about a pastor in Las Vegas who saw a young man standing on a street corner weeping profusely. The pastor went to the young man and offered to help. The young man was from New York, in town for a few days to "have a good time." He decided he would gamble a little. He won some, then lost it all. He didn't even have the money to get back home so he could return to work. Sadly, that story has been repeated countless times in "Sin City."

Take in the whole picture. No fellow gamblers out there offered a hand. Not one casino owner tried to help him out of his misery. No card dealers or pit bosses were out there with him. They had taken all he had and cared nothing about what happened once he exited their glimmering palaces. That is precisely what Satan does to all who dare to build on anything less than Jesus Christ.

Here's what I want to know: How do I build a life that will stand? How do I construct a sturdy, long-standing house? According to Jesus, two things are essential.

First, we must hear the Word of God. That means a lot more than just showing up on an occasional Sunday. Many of us have gone to hundreds, if not thousands, of church services in our lifetime. Sadly, we can't recall most of what was said. The first step in hearing is understanding—grasping what we have been told. Nothing is as vital to survival as grasping and understanding God's Word. No emotional upheaval can replace it. No spiritual experience can substitute for it. God's Word in our lives is indispensable to withstand the storms!

Second, Jesus moves from hearing to doing. It is not enough to only hear and understand what was said. We must "do" the Word of God. Even when we don't want to because our flesh screams otherwise, we must obey God's Word to survive.

Do you remember what Jesus taught us in this great sermon? Remember what He taught about adultery? It's not enough to abstain from having an affair. To survive, we must strive for a pure mind that never entertains the thought of such an action. He also taught us to give, which means we must open our hearts and bank accounts and release some of the money we have worked so hard to earn. Additionally, we are to be such trustworthy people that we don't have to back up our promises with an oath. We are to live in such a way that people trust us. The list goes on. If we are to build on Christ the Rock, our obedience must be our building material. Only such a life can withstand the storms.

Chilling Words

Rather than end with a feel-good illustration that makes us want to come back next week, Jesus leaves us to ponder one of the most chilling passages in all His recorded words:

> "Not everyone who says to Me, 'Lord, Lord,' shall enter the kingdom of heaven, but he who does the will of My Father in heaven. Many will say to Me in that day, 'Lord, Lord, have we not prophesied in Your name, cast out demons in Your name, and done many wonders in Your name?' And then I will declare to them, 'I never knew you; depart from Me, you who practice lawlessness!'" (Matthew 7:21–23).

I can't think of a more frightening scene than this one. This is not a parable but a future event. He was clear and to the point. A day is coming when many people will stand before Him in judgment and receive the terrible awakening that He *"never knew"* them.

Many will point out this passage follows His message about false teachers and how to recognize them. Granted, that's true, but it's haunting to think people believed they knew Christ because of what took place in their ministry.

According to Jesus, it is possible to preach many sermons about Him but never be known by Him. We can push others toward the gates of Heaven without entering them ourselves. Amazingly, we can witness miracles as we pray for people in His name but not be registered in His book. I shudder when considering the shocking truth He spoke.

Decades ago, I was honored to know a great man of God named F. M. Sides. Brother Sides was a retired Church of God pastor and leader extraordinaire in Alabama. By the time I came to know him, he was well into the latter part of his life. Being a boy preacher, I would chat with him about what he read and how he developed his preaching.

One night, F. M. told his wife he was convinced Jesus was about to come back, and he wanted to be sure he was ready.

I still remember thinking, *If F. M. Sides is not ready, I don't have a chance!*

From what I can tell, F. M. made it in. I even think he made it in with a flourish. However, we will all one day have to face the issue of whether we are known in Heaven by the Son of God. In the greatest sermon ever, Jesus provided two ways to evaluate our association with Him. It's not the time to look at anyone else right now. This is time for each of us to do some self-evaluation.

The first way deals with doing "the will of My Father" versus practicing "lawlessness" (Matthew 7:23), which means refusing to submit to any law. The specific law here is the will of God. Jesus is very pointed here, so don't miss what He says. Eternity hangs in the balance for everyone on this issue. If we refuse to follow the will of God, we are practicing lawlessness and headed for an eternity without the Lord.

Here's where this gets personal and downright scary. In ministry, I am judged by most people on how I preach. Others judge me based on how I did or did not provide an aspect of pastoral care. The leadership of a ministry might judge me on my administrative skills. Yet, none of those things factor into Jesus' judgment. His approach is simple: *Did I submit my life to His will?*

I could die with you thinking I was a great pastor, a great preacher, a great administrator, a great toilet-bowl cleaner, or whatever. Yet when I stand before Him, if I fail this one test, I will hear the horrible words, "Depart! I never knew you!"

Some will respond, "Ah, so we can work our way into Heaven." No. A thousand times, no! There is no way it can be done. If one can work miracles, surely that would suffice. Yet, such is not the case. We can, however, work our way out of

Heaven. If we live like we do not want to go to Heaven, God will not force the celestial city upon us.

How, then, shall we enter? Who can know for sure they are living an everlasting life? I once had a church member come to me in despair. He had read and heard the comparison made by Jesus about being more righteous than the Pharisees. It bothered him, and he felt like he was not good enough to get into Heaven. I said I shared the same fear, but then I gave him Jesus' second way to evaluate if we are known by Him.

First, it is not *who* you are; it is about *whose* you are. Make sure you belong to Jesus, lock, stock, and barrel. Second, it's not what you do; it's who you know. Make sure you are walking in surrender and submission to Him. Third, it is not how great you can become; it's how broken you can get. Make sure you are humbled and stay before Him all the time. Fourth, keep returning to this masterful sermon's beginning. It is the foundation stone of His kingdom: *"Blessed are the poor in spirit, for theirs is the Kingdom of Heaven" (Matthew 5:3).*

Don't be afraid to keep running back to Him, shouting your bankruptcy and inadequacy. That is how the vastness of His kingdom becomes available to you. The power needed to sustain you is included in that Kingdom. Lean completely on what He gives, and Judgment Day will bring you no harm.

Those who know Christ and are known by Him will have no fear in that day, for the One making the judgment will be their close friend.

SERMON OUTLINE

Introduction: Every great sermon has a rousing conclusion that grabs your attention and drives home the truth. The Sermon on the Mount is no exception. When everyone in attendance that day was gathering up their belongings, Jesus added an "Oh, by the way" conclusion. These are some of the scariest words Jesus uttered.

1. CONSTRUCTION PROJECTS
   a. Comparisons
   b. Continuation
   c. Commonalities
2. COMMENTARY BY PAUL
   a. Watchful
   b. Word-built
   c. Working Out Your Salvation
3. CHILLING WORDS
   a. Shocking!
   b. Submission
   c. Standing in the Day

Conclusion: Keep running back to the first bedrock truth Jesus taught (Matthew 5:3). The vastness of His Kingdom becomes available to the most bankrupt among us when we admit our failures before Him. The ability to keep us in that day is included in the unlimited resources of His Kingdom.

STUDY QUESTIONS

1. What do incidents such as an apartment building collapse say about the necessity of a strong foundation?
2. How can you build a strong foundation in life? What materials have you used for your foundation in Jesus?
3. Storms come to everyone. Talk about surviving a physical or spiritual storm and how the foundation of your life in Jesus enabled you to have victory.
4. How does the fact that Dietrich Bonhoeffer spent time preparing a manuscript for a sermon just hours before his death impact you? Do you need to invest more time carefully studying God's Word?
5. Can your foundation withstand false teachers? What prominent false teachings exist today?
6. Examine your heart and life. What will you experience on that day when you stand before Jesus? Why?
7. Are there areas in your life that need to be surrendered to Christ? If so, are you willing to lay them at His feet now?

5

A GOOD ROMAN

Now when He concluded all His sayings in the hearing of the people, He entered Capernaum. And a certain centurion's servant, who was dear to him, was sick and ready to die. So when he heard about Jesus, he sent elders of the Jews to Him, pleading with Him to come and heal his servant. [4] And when they came to Jesus, they begged Him earnestly, saying that the one for whom He should do this was deserving, "for he loves our nation, and has built us a synagogue." Then Jesus went with them. And when He was already not far from the house, the centurion sent friends to Him, saying to Him, "Lord, do not trouble Yourself, for I am not worthy that You should enter under my roof. Therefore I did not even think myself worthy to come to You. But say the word, and my servant will be healed. For I also am a man placed under authority, having soldiers under me. And I say to one, 'Go,' and he goes; and to another, 'Come,' and he comes; and to my servant, 'Do this,' and he does it." When Jesus heard these things, He marveled at him, and turned around and said to the crowd that followed Him, "I say to you, I have not found such great faith, not even in Israel!" And those who were sent, returning to the house, found the servant well who had been sick (Luke 7:1–10).

I love to watch people. It's amazing what you can learn by silently paying attention to what people say and by observing how they conduct themselves. In fact, a great amount can be learned about someone you have never met by a few moments of keen observation. Before us now is a Roman, a man I call a good Roman. I never met him, but I know some important facts about his life. What's more, he has shown each of us a way to move into the presence of Jesus and encounter something extraordinary.

Having finished the retreat where He preached the world's greatest sermon, Jesus and His entourage came down from the peace and solitude of the mountain and once more entered the hustle and bustle of the city. Itinerant ministry again began to place demands on the Master.

The moment He entered the city, Jesus was met by a delegation of Jewish elders who presented a strange request. They asked Him to come to the home of someone they did not like and do something gracious for someone else for whom they cared very little. The elders, amazingly, asked Jesus to do something good for a Roman.

That doesn't sound so out of place for us, but it was unheard of back then. The Jews hated the Romans. Their visceral contempt is comparable to the seething hatred exhibited today toward anything "Western" by Muslim extremists in the war-torn areas of the world. It was palpable and existed on every corner.

There is little wonder that such animus existed. The Romans were not, after all, the most compassionate of people. They pretty much did what they wanted, when they wanted, to whom they wanted, and powerless Israel had to sit there and take it. Perhaps you were like me after viewing the film *The Passion of the Christ.* I watched in pain as the soldiers acted like brute beasts when they slaughtered the Lamb of God. I walked out with words such as *brutal, savage,* and *rabid dogs* rattling around in my brain. The Romans were often snobbish murderers who lived on the law of "might makes right." They demonstrated a style of life which, when looking back, demanded their extermination, not examination. Yet, here I stand, calling on us to pay careful attention to a Roman. To do less would cause us to miss one of the greatest lessons about touching Jesus found in all the Bible.

Unexpected People

Maybe I need instructions. After all, before I throw all Romans into one disgusting pile, I might need to take a step back from my emotionally driven condemnation and carefully evaluate this man. After all, that's what I want Jesus to do for me. And the deeper I dig into this man's life, the better he becomes. In fact, by the time I am finished, I hope I can come close to this Roman's standing with Jesus.

We are told he was a centurion. That's a ranking like a military captain today. He had one hundred men under his command, hence the term *centurion.* Interestingly, every time a centurion is mentioned in the Bible, the individual is cast positively. Standing at the feet of the crucified Son of God, a centurion declared Him to be the "Son of God" (Mark 15:39). Cornelius, who called for Simon Peter, was a centurion (Acts 10:1). Julius, a centurion, guarded the life of Paul (27:1). Only one centurion is cast in a negative light because he was on the verge of scourging Paul. Even then, he was only doing his task. When he heard Paul was a Roman citizen, he stopped the procedure to save Paul from illegal punishment (22:25-26). In the quest for fairness, I must step back from my prejudice against all Roman soldiers in the time of Jesus and admit there were some good men in their ranks.

I can tell you some personal things about the centurion in Luke 7, though our paths have never crossed. He was a religious man. I know this because he gave the Jews money to build a synagogue. Romans were not taught to do such things. They were to keep themselves above issues such as local religions. Yet this man saw something in Jehovah that intrigued him. He came to the issue with an open heart.

He was also a wealthy man. If you give enough to build a church, even a small church, you are blessed with ample funds. Resources were his, and he was willing to invest them. He was a Roman whose religion had touched every area of his life. It got into his wallet, hence the new church building. Sure, he could have had an ulterior motive for building the new church. Maybe he wanted his name prominently displayed. Perhaps he had cut a deal with the locals to build it so they would cut down on protests and make his job easier. It could have been his knowledge that investing some money in a local project made for good optics. All those are possibilities, but something else convinces me this Roman had been deeply affected by his religion. He cared about someone other than himself!

A close examination of the story reveals a great deal about him: *"And a certain centurion's servant, who was dear to him, was sick and ready to die"* (Luke 7:2).

This was not the observation of Luke. It was not an addition to the story to make things sound better. These words flowed forth from the lips of a group of people describing the situation. They used a word for the servant that was the normal word for a slave. In fact, the centurion used this term when speaking of this individual. But as the story progresses, the centurion speaks for himself and uses a word a father would employ in describing his son. The Jews called this man a servant; the centurion called him a son. The Jews who had the Word of God and were supposed to be caring and gentle called him a simple servant. This Roman, accustomed to violent battles, used tender, endearing language. Compassion and mercy had found a lodging place deep within his Roman heart. When we put together a religion that bends a man and makes him pliable in the hands of God and a man who is willing to be bent, we have a combination that our God can greatly use.

Watching these events unfold, I learned a great deal from this man. Apart from Jesus, he was the centerpiece of the story. Our focus is not on the sick young man. He may tug at our heartstrings, but the lesson is seeing this good man moving the great heart of Jesus. Oh, that I could discover how to walk in his footsteps!

If you have a need, learn to walk like this good Roman. If you are trying to find a path that leads you closer to Jesus, retrace the footsteps of this blessed man. If you need a miracle, perhaps in your family, maybe in your heart, you can't do better than to mimic the actions of this good Roman. Paying attention to him and catching a glimpse of his heart will show us the passageway that leads to the inner sanctum of God's blessing.

Understanding Power

The reason the Jews implored Jesus to do something for the centurion was simple. They thought he deserved it. They wanted Jesus to bless him because he had done some nice things for them.

If we have any hopes of coming into the presence of God and being blessed, we must come to a firm understanding of the way things work in His Kingdom. There is one hard and fast rule, and it is universal in application. No one deserves anything from God. Yes, that means the best of the best. Paul made that very clear. No flesh, no one, no character, will ever revel or *"glory in His [God's] presence"* (1 Corinthians 1:29).

There will never be a time when any human will stand before God and say, "I earned this blessing." No matter what you do or don't do, you never get on the "God-owes-me" side of the debt ledger. Forget the idea that tithing means God owes you anything. While the tithe is His, so is the other 90 percent. Drop the notion that you put forth all the effort to get to some arena and waited in line for some healing evangelist (whatever that is) to pray over you means God owes you healing. He may well heal you, but it will be due to His grace, not your effort. Remember, God owns you, so He can do with you what He wants. Lay aside the wishful thinking that if you can pray loud enough, do enough, give enough, sacrifice enough, or *whatever* enough that God will say, "I better get busy with that guy, or he is going to get ahead of Me, and I will have to buy him lunch!"

Read the Bible and pay attention. The Lord was going to the man's house, and the man's need was going to be met, but it had nothing to do with the fact he had built the Jews a house of worship. It all came about because of the man's understanding and faith in the authority and power of Jesus.

Without jumping too far ahead, pause and take a deep breath. Many may feel as if they have been shoved aside and abandoned. It might be feeling like Jesus overlooked you because you are not part of the "in" crowd at church. It's easy to hear all the stuff people talk about doing for Jesus and think, *I don't have a chance around here*. We must come to grips with the fact that all those parameters have nothing to do with His power. There is only one reason God does anything for us: He loves us. He loves us so much that He ripped time and space asunder and allowed His only Son to be inserted into our broken and lonely world. He did this so He could touch us, no matter who we are. He did it so He could move mightily in our lives, regardless of who we are.

So, stop worrying about what you have done or not done. Stop sitting back and allowing the glory of God to pass you by because you think you have not done enough. Reach out to Him with your emptiness in full display and discover His amazing love and power.

The Immense Power of Jesus' Words

The statement made by the centurion is remarkable (Luke 7:7-8). I want to ask him where He learned it. He displayed an insight into the power of Jesus unlike anyone else had ever shown. He grasped truth about Jesus that many of us who have hung around church for decades still miss. He somehow knew all that Jesus had to do in his situation was release a word, and his beloved servant would be healed. There was no need for calisthenics, no call for gestures of grandeur—just a word spoken by Jesus, and all would be well.

He understood because he was a devoted Roman centurion and knew how power flowed up and down the chain of command. In his rank, he had those above him who issued orders. Because they had been issued by his superiors, he obeyed. Similarly, when he gave orders to those serving beneath him, they obeyed equally. It was all a matter of authority and rank. In our country, one person sits at the top of a massive military. The President of the United States is the Commander in Chief of all military forces. When the President issues an order, even four-star generals who are accustomed to absolute obedience and deference from all others must jump to attention and obey. . . or else. They might not agree with the order, but they are duty-bound to obey. They do so because they understand the power of the office.

This good Roman grasped the amazing things that happen when authority is displayed. He understood who Jesus was and the awesome power residing in Him. He didn't have a religious education like the Jewish leaders. He had no theological training like the priests. Yet, he realized the power and authority in the words of Jesus.

Many of us immersed in life and church have lost that vision and connection with the power in the words of our Lord. In case your senses have been dulled a bit, let me remind you of a few things. Read the words of the resurrected Lord, fresh from conquering death, hell, and the grave. Let them reverberate through your spirit as you take in the amazing power He boasts: *"All authority has been given to Me in heaven and on earth"* (Matthew 28:18).

If that is not enough, let this next Scripture soak deep into your spirit. Say aloud these inspiring words of hope and power as you face the battles of life: *"I am He who lives, and was dead, and behold, I am alive forevermore. Amen. And I have the keys of Hades and of Death"* (Revelation 1:18).

Jesus is not dead. He is not weak, anemic, or fearful. He is not lost out there somewhere. He is not insensitive to you and your needs. He is not hiding until the big, bad devil decides to retire. He is in Heaven, bringing to pass the Father's will. If a Roman soldier, looking at Jesus standing along the road, can somehow come to that conclusion and recognize His power, why can't we look to Him in faith and come to that same conclusion? Jesus can speak His word, and suddenly, all things are possible.

Matthew's account gives us an insight into the interaction between Jesus and the Roman soldier:

> "Lord, my servant is lying at home paralyzed, dreadfully tormented." And Jesus said to him, "I will come and heal him." The centurion answered and said, "Lord, I am not worthy that You should come under my roof. But only speak a word, and my servant will be healed. For I also am a man under authority, having soldiers under me. And I say to this one, 'Go,' and he goes; and to another, 'Come,' and he comes; and to my servant, 'Do this,' and he does it" (Matthew 8:6-9).

What an act of faith! By what he said and did, the centurion positioned himself for a move of God. I have often wondered how many mighty moves and miracles of God I have missed because I had fixed in my mind exactly when and how God was supposed to show up. I fear that most of us who have been around the church for a while have a rigid set of parameters by which we expect God to make Himself known. We come to church with preconceived ideas about how the Lord is going to save someone. We think we know, in advance, what God is going to do if we are going to be blessed. If those boxes are not checked off per our requirements, there will be no move of God today.

I think we have lost something. We have somehow lost our willingness to demonstrate faith—not just talk about faith or even teach about it. We seem reluctant to demonstrate faith in God's power.

The good Roman demonstrated faith by not uttering the "death rattle" sentence we often hear: *It's always been done this way.* He was not cemented in a position that demanded things be done exactly as before. As far as he knew, Jesus had done some amazing things, but only when He had been right there. The centurion expressed his faith in Jesus doing something no one had ever seen before and in an unfamiliar way.

He also demonstrated faith when Jesus simply uttered a few words. To him, a word was all he needed. No second-guessing. No, "Well, maybe you should come home with me after all." Jesus spoke, and the centurion went home. Case closed.

When we get into the position where Jesus speaks, we must move. We must respond. We must make room for Him to work in our lives and then let Him do that work.

Jesus *"marveled"* at this kind of faith demonstration (Matthew 8:10). He looked at all the people gathered and told them this man's demonstration of faith was the most amazing thing He had seen. No one in Israel could top the faith this guy demonstrated.

You and I marvel at great buildings. Jesus wasn't even interested in the house of worship this guy built for the Jews. We get caught up in money and are swayed when a rich guy gives away a lot of resources. Jesus never flinched at this guy's money. We fall over ourselves when someone of notoriety shows up in church. Jesus wasn't remotely impressed by the centurion's rank. But his faith—Jesus stepped back and admired it like a prized jewel. Jesus is searching for someone facing an impossible situation today and looking loss in the eye. Someone with the nerve to declare to all that rises in opposition, "You are nothing compared to my Lord" (see Matthew 21:21).

Unusual Faith

Perhaps you feel like you don't fit in. Maybe you were not raised in church and have more questions than answers.

You may not know the jargon, and the songs may be unfamiliar. Perhaps you are not accustomed to the way we "do" church and don't know what everything means. It might even be a little scary to you. If that is the case, join the club! But don't let that make you shrink back into the corner and leave without touching the Master. If you are interested at all in a divine encounter, your problems have placed you in the right place.

If we are not careful, some of us old-timers are going to miss the whole show, while some who don't know the Holy Ghost from Hollywood ghosts will witness a great move of God. That's tough language, but that's what Jesus said: *"Many will come from east and west, and sit down with Abraham, Isaac, and Jacob in the kingdom of heaven. But the sons of the Kingdom will be cast out into outer darkness. There will be weeping and gnashing of teeth"* (Matthew 8:11-12).

The Jews thought the Messiah would show up and host a great banquet to which only they were invited. Everyone else was out of luck. It never occurred to them that outsiders might get invited. In fact, the idea that this Roman would be included was scandalous.

You would think the sons of the Kingdom would get it. You would think those of us who have been around the things of God for decades would be first in line. Yet sometimes, we take the Lord and Master for granted and develop a rebellious and stubborn nature, and as a result, we miss Him when He wants to move powerfully in our lives.

Then, from out of nowhere, some Roman centurion shows up and reminds us anyone can come to God. He shakes the cobwebs off our faith and reaffirms there is nothing too hard for God. His actions scream that, regardless of someone's past, they can rush into the presence of God and receive His touch.

You may not feel like it, but you can be blessed. Some of the *"sons of the Kingdom"* may have written you off and convinced you that God does not care for you. Their opinions mean nothing. You can push by them and experience His glory in your life. Once there, you never know what may be waiting for you. Follow the steps of this good Roman. The amazing answer you seek will be found as you bump into the Son of God along the way.

SERMON OUTLINE

Introduction: Let's meet one of the many characters who had a brief encounter with the Master. If you enjoy watching people, this will not only be a learning experience, it will be a pleasant experience. We are going to meet, of all things, a good Roman. Very few Romans are shown in a positive light by the Gospel writers, but this man is an exception. In fact, by following the same pathway he walked, you and I can have a similarly powerful encounter with Jesus.

1. UNEXPECTED PEOPLE
   a. Centurion in the Roman Army
   b. Centered Lifestyle in Religion
   c. Compassionate in Relationships
2. UNDERSTANDING POWER
   a. No One Will Glory in God's Presence
   b. Nothing Can Compete with Jesus' Words
   c. Never Minimize a Demonstration of Faith
3. UNUSUAL FAITH
   a. Fitting in
   b. Failing to Receive
   c. Finding Your Answer

Conclusion: You may not feel like it, but you can be blessed. Some may have written you off, but their opinions do not matter. Press by them, as did this good Roman, and walk into the presence of Jesus. Who knows what might be awaiting you there?

STUDY QUESTIONS

1. How does it strike you that a man such as this one—a soldier in the Roman Army—was able to have a powerful encounter with Jesus? Is there any class of people who are outside His reach?
2. Describe someone who has come to Christ you never thought you would see serving Him. What made you think they were beyond salvation? How were they won to the Lord? Is there something we need to be doing to bring other similar people to Christ?
3. Do you feel God owes you something? Is there any way we can get in His debt?
4. Do the words of Jesus still carry power today? Do you surrender your life to His words and teachings?
5. Faith on display might express what this good Roman did before the crowd. How might we put our faith on display today?
6. How can you build your faith in God?
7. Have you ever missed something from God because you failed to act on His Word? How can you prevent that from occurring in the future?

6

WHO DOES HE THINK HE IS?

> Now it happened, the day after, that He went into a city called Nain; and many of His disciples went with Him, and a large crowd. And when He came near the gate of the city, behold, a dead man was being carried out, the only son of his mother; and she was a widow. And a large crowd from the city was with her. When the Lord saw her, He had compassion on her and said to her, "Do not weep." Then He came and touched the open coffin, and those who carried him stood still. And He said, "Young man, I say to you, arise." So he who was dead sat up and began to speak. And He presented him to his mother. Then fear came upon all, and they glorified God, saying, "A great prophet has risen up among us"; and, "God has visited His people." And this report about Him went throughout all Judea and all the surrounding region (Luke 7:11–17).

This story is one of my favorites. It shines a spotlight on Jesus' character and ability to touch our lives. However, some scholars seek to attack this story because it is mentioned only one time in the Gospels. They seem to feel as if God must repeat Himself for them to agree on authenticity. However, there is no greater representation of the entirety of the Biblical message than this short account from the life of Jesus?

After healing the centurion's servant, Jesus and His entourage made the eighteen-mile trek from Capernaum to the small village of Nain. As the Lord approached the outskirts of the small town, there was a traffic jam. On one side was Jesus and the ever-swelling crowd His presence drew. On the other, coming out of the city, was a throng pressing along in a funeral march. Those with Jesus would later discover a young man had died, leaving a heartbroken mother who was not only grieving but also husbandless. She was in deep trouble, and those walking with her knew it. That sad stream of broken humanity was on the way to disposing of the remains of this woman's only hope.

This mother had heard the earth-shattering words, "He's gone." In typical Middle Eastern fashion, she ripped her clothes in sorrow and despair. Her son's body had been laid out and prepared for burial. His remains had been washed and his hair cut. The body was then anointed with oils and wrapped in the best cloth the woman could afford. After some lamenting, her only child would be buried outside the city. Her hopes, dreams, and life were being taken out and put in the ground, hidden from view.

On the way to the cemetery, there would be crying, singing, music, and a lot of wailing and travail. Alfred Edershiem pointed out, "It was deemed the duty of the poorest Jew on the death of his wife to provide at least two flutes and one mourner."[1] We can be assured this funeral contained more than that. This whole area must have been moved with compassion for this woman.

Suddenly, the two large crowds collided. One was going outside the city to mourn the loss of life and joy. The other was coming into the city following the Lord of life and hope. One crowd was singing a funeral dirge; the other crowd was shouting victory around the One who had power over sickness and death.

---

[1] Alfred Edershiem, *The Life and Times of Jesus the Messiah* (Grand Rapids: Eerdmans, 1971), 555.

One crowd was carrying a dead body; the other crowd was following the One destined to conquer death for all men.[2] As the two crowds were merging into one shoving mass of humanity, Jesus did the unthinkable.

> *"Then He came and touched the open coffin, and those who carried him stood still. And He said, 'Young man, I say to you, arise'"* (Luke 7:14).

He moved toward the group carrying the boy's body and stopped the funeral procession. The text is clear. They did not come to Jesus; He deliberately moved toward them. Then, to everyone's amazement, He stopped a funeral and touched a dead body. That was one of the ultimate taboos. Jews were forbidden to touch dead bodies.[3] However, Jesus was not concerned with the defilement affecting Him. As we shall see, death had much more to fear from Him than it could ever hurl at the Master!

I don't have any problem imagining the crowd, the professional onlookers, and maybe even some of the disciples gawking and asking themselves, *Who does He think He is? What does He think He is doing?* Even in our increasingly secular age, stopping a funeral is still considered a no-no.

Think for a moment about all we do for funerals. We hire police officers to stop traffic and ignore red lights. Funeral processions are given priority by everyone on the road. Cars pull over and headlights turn on because most people give the

---

[2] Revelation 1:17-18 makes it clear that Jesus has already conquered death. We have nothing to fear!

[3] Leviticus 21:1 establishes the distance for the sons of Aaron to keep between themselves and the corpses of others. Only those of closest relations were to be touched. The high priest was given a further command: He must not defile himself with any dead body (v. 11).

right-of-way to the procession out of deference to the family. You just do not stop funerals.

After a funeral service I conducted in Bessemer, Alabama, we were headed to the cemetery, much like the crowd encountered by Jesus. The funeral director came up to my car and told me the lead car was unable to start. I would have to be the lead car in the long procession. I agreed—no problem on my part.

We started out of the funeral home parking lot when it dawned on me: I had no idea where we were going for the burial! Slowly creeping out, I scanned left and right. To my relief, there was a police officer about five blocks up to my left, holding traffic for us. As I crawled toward him, I finally caught his eye. Holding up my hands, I mouthed, "I don't know which way to go." He grinned and gave me a "turn left" signal. So far, so good. My next dilemma compounded my angst. A few blocks down was a five-lane street. I had to turn, and there was no smiling police officer to help me. I had a fifty-fifty chance, so I turned left. The funeral director didn't start blaring his horn at me, so I had guessed correctly. Finally, I was able to catch his eyes in my rear-view mirror. I exaggerated my speech, telling him I did not know where we were going. He started belly laughing. I wasn't all that entertained, and he indicated where to turn next. We made it on time, barely.

Another funeral procession gone wrong occurred when the parade of cars came upon an accident at a busy intersection. Looking back, it seems comical. I had to divert through an intersection and cut through a parking lot in front of a grocery store. People came out and stared at us like we were crazy. I have often wondered if some shopper with a cart filled with not-good-for-you foods paused and wondered if they were being sent a message. But we did not stop!

Yet, stopping a funeral is precisely what Jesus did. You can call it unthinkable, unsocial, even uncouth. On that day, Jesus decided the funeral had gone far enough, so the Giver of Life decided to rain on the parade of power held by death.

Everyone had to be asking, "Who does He think He is?" That is a legitimate question. I want to know if the dentist working on my teeth is qualified. When I have surgery, I want to know the surgeon graduated from medical school. When I am involved in some legal proceedings, I want to know my attorney passed the bar exam. More importantly, I want to know that the person teaching me eternal things actually knows something about the Bible. Who and what you are mean everything when things get serious. And this scene of life and death was as serious as anything could ever be. *Who did He think He was?* That's important, but not nearly as important as who He really was.

A Common Man

Jesus was far removed from the aloof, uncaring, above-the-rest-of-us character some try to make Him out to be. He was very much like the rest of us. He likely had stepped aside to watch other funeral processions, and He perhaps had walked in some of them, including for Joseph, his earthly father.

Jesus was there with them and among them. He wasn't being carried in a velvet-draped carriage. He was part of them and part of the crowd. Never let this be lost on you. He did not sit in splendor and demand that we claw into His presence. He put on flesh and became one of us. Far from demanding that we get our acts together to come around Him, He became like us, "*yet without sin*" (Hebrews 4:15).

Jesus is holy. He is the Judge before whom all must stand and give account. While He is building a place for us in glory, He was born in a cattle pen. He sculpted the universe as the

Creator, but He also did woodwork as a boy in Joseph's workshop. He is the King of kings, but He also lived as a poor, itinerant preacher. While kings of this earth who bow before Him are accepted by Him, so are those who live in cardboard boxes. Millionaires praise Him, as do impoverished families. He is one of "us," regardless of what "us" you mention.

He understands what makes us tick. When it comes to our struggles, inner pain, and intense disappointments, He gets it. *"For we do not have a High Priest who cannot sympathize with our weaknesses, but was in all points tempted as we are, yet without sin. Let us therefore come boldly to the throne of grace, that we may obtain mercy and find grace to help in time of need"* (Hebrews 4:15–16).

Because He was tempted like me, I can tell Him exactly how I feel. I can express to Him what I am going through. He knows because He lived it.

That means so much to me because I tend to struggle with the slightest of mishaps. I have a tendency to spiral downward when things strike me in the wrong way. I think this poor woman and I have something in common, for life had stung her so badly she was caught in a maelstrom of despair. I doubt she noticed Jesus was there.

Nain means "pleasant place." Her town was indeed a pleasant place to live. Archeological digs have revealed Biblical Nain was a small town with walls and towers. It was a safe place to live. They discovered it was filled with gardens and fragrant fruit trees. Near the city were hills covered in evergreen trees, with Mount Tabor rising in the distance. Turn the other way, and the splendor of Mount Hermon's snowcapped peaks protruded heavenward. It was a special place, and now Jesus was there

. . . but she was caught up in her pain and saw none of the glory surrounding her.

Despite all my years of training and studying, there are times when, like this woman, life crushes me and a dull numbness takes over. Things are good around me, but I am so fixated on my pain that I don't notice them. Worse yet, I can become attached to my pain and fail to notice the One who can make things different.

How shameful I forget He is with me. How much pain do I endure because I forget He knows how I feel? It is my loss to become so self-absorbed that I forget He knows about my temptations. My life is much better when I remember He can take me through to victory. For all who share the valley of painful obsessions with me, hear me well: He gets it. He knows. If we stop the procession of pain for a moment, He will inject Himself and bring hope and healing.

A Compassionate Man

"When the Lord saw her, He had compassion on her, and said to her, 'Do not weep'" (Luke 7:13).

When I was thirteen years old, my father died suddenly on December 18. One week before Christmas, my life shattered. I can vividly recall standing in front of his casket, broken and weeping. A woman walked up and rebuked me. She demanded that I stop crying. Being a young, crushed kid, I don't remember what I said or did. I will add this: She should be thankful I was a confused and crushed thirteen-year-old because she would not like what she would hear if she tried that today!

Ah, but when Jesus walked over and told the woman, "Lady, stop crying," it was totally different. I do not know what drove that woman so many years ago to assault me in front of my father's casket, but I do know what prompted Jesus. We are told He was moved with "compassion." It was a deep, visceral reaction to everything He saw. Every time you come across this word in the New Testament associated with Jesus, it is always the result of a personal encounter. Jesus ran into something that tore at His great heart and moved Him to do something. The profuse weeping of the woman, the sight of the boy in the wicker basket, and the moaning of the crowd all combined to create a sight that drove deep into Jesus' heart.

There was nothing the woman could offer Jesus to motivate Him. The state of the boy was not the motivating factor. Instead, it was compassion for someone with nothing to offer Him that moved His majestic heart to action. We tend to forget the image of our God and the passion He carries for those who bring nothing to the table.

> *"The Lord watches over the strangers; He relieves the fatherless and widow"* (Psalm 146:9). *"A father of the fatherless, a defender of widows, is God in His holy habitation"* (68:5).

Widows and orphans have nothing to offer Him, but He deeply cares for them. You may have nothing to offer God today. You may feel useless and worthless. That matters not to Him. You can be marginalized by everyone and have zero hope for the future. If so, you are a prime candidate for Jesus' compassion.

Sadly, we church members often have a difficult time handling the fact Jesus has compassion on people . . . other than us, of course! We, if not careful, will adopt a worldly point of view. We replace His compassion with the idea that *"they made their bed, let them sleep in it."* It stuns some of us that the alcoholic who has guzzled liquor all his life and destroyed his body attracts Jesus' compassion. We are perplexed when the drug addict who persisted despite all the warnings and used his family and friends is a prime target for Jesus' love. The adulterer who ignored his family and commitments and instead followed his own lusts is sought by Christ's compassion. The thief who stole from under his boss's nose and the liar who keeps digging deeper and deeper are loved by the Savior.

We are able to look the other way, developing a "they are getting what they deserve" theology, usually forgetting we were rescued from a pit. Meanwhile, the Master is moved with compassion toward them. Who does He think He is? The answer is simple. He is the One who can make a difference in the life of anyone, regardless of what they have done or are now doing. When a woman caught in adultery was dragged before Him, He looked at her without flinching and said, "You are forgiven!" While the religious group was foaming at the mouth for justice, Jesus was moved with compassion. Nothing about Him has changed. Today, He embodies compassion for the broken and shattered lives around us.

A Conquering Man

"Then He came and touched the open coffin, and those who carried him stood still. And He said, 'Young man, I say to you, arise.' So he who was dead sat up and began to speak. And He presented him to his mother" (Luke 7:14-15).

Jesus walked over to the bier and said, "Boy, get up." There was no long prayer, no plaintive request. He spoke, and it happened. This should not surprise us. When Jesus speaks, the attacks of the enemy are reversed.

When a centurion told Jesus his beloved servant was at the point of death, Jesus told him, *"'Go your way; and as you have believed, so let it be done for you.' And his servant was healed that same hour"* (Matthew 8:13).

There was no great struggle. No great fuss. In fact, there was not a direct command. Jesus told a man to go home and apparently sent a thought to a disease-ridden body to be healed. Both responded to the actions of this conquering Man.

While it is one thing to prevent someone from dying, it is altogether different to force death out of a body and restore life. I would have loved to witness this one. Can you imagine what Satan thought when that boy jumped out of that basket? Can you imagine the shock of the men carrying the body to the grave when the basket started shaking and the corpse began chattering? I think they dropped that basket, corpse and all, and scattered. That scene has amazing news for us. If Jesus can conquer death, He can handle anything life throws our way.

There is something here beyond the immediate need He met. After all, there were others who had lost loved ones. Why did Jesus not resurrect all their family members? Why does Jesus not empty cemeteries and put funeral homes out of business today? The reason is simple: It is not yet time for that to happen. This amazing incident points to the day when the Conqueror will step to the edge of eternity and invade every burial ground, plunge into every ocean and sea, and do the same thing He did just outside Nain. Jesus was demonstrating His unconquerable power, even over death, when He emptied that wicker basket. Mediate on the comforting words of 1 Thessalonians 4:13-17:

> But I do not want you to be ignorant, brethren, concerning those who have fallen asleep, lest you sorrow as others who have no hope. For if we believe that Jesus died and rose again, even so God will bring with Him those who sleep in Jesus. For this we say to you by the word of the Lord, that we who are alive and remain until the coming of the

> Lord will by no means precede those who are asleep. For the Lord Himself will descend from heaven with a shout, with the voice of an archangel, and with the trumpet of God. And the dead in Christ will rise first. Then we who are alive and remain shall be caught up together with them in the clouds to meet the Lord in the air. And thus we shall always be with the Lord.

Have we relegated that passage to something we occasionally read at funerals to offer comfort and hope to the grieving survivors? It is so much more. It explains what happened in a staggering moment outside Nain when the conquering Man decided to show the reach of His power. At some moment, perhaps in the next one after you read these words, the Conqueror will have a trumpet blasted, and He will invade death's domain once more. This time, it will not be singular but universal. This time, it will not be temporary (for this man died once more and remains so today), but it will be eternal as we will forever be with the ultimate Conqueror.

Too many of us have given up on our conquering Lord. Who does He think He is? He thinks He is Lord of all. He knows all power in Heaven and earth has been given to Him. He is seated at the right hand of God today to pray for us.

When the widow's son was raised, the onlookers "*were all filled with awe and praised God. 'A great prophet has appeared among us,' they said. "God has come to help his people'*" (Luke 7:16 NIV).

Throw your life on Jesus and see if He is who He says He is. That's what the family of Rich Sprenkel did. He was a rebellious teenager and student at Chico State University in Chico, California. Coming home from a drinking party, Rich swerved to miss a dog in the road. His soft-topped Jeep flipped and landed on him. His neck hit the curb, and a large wrench penetrated his skull. His pelvis was broken in four places and his head was split open from his ear to the top of his head. Bystanders kept him alive through mouth-to-mouth resuscitation until paramedics arrived.

Once they got him to a hospital, X-rays revealed his spinal column was severed, his neck broken in four places, and his vertebrae were separated. His parents, strong believers in Jesus, started praying. So did many others. The doctors told them the sad news. It was probable that their son would slip away at any moment. If he did survive, he would be a vegetable, nothing more.

But the family kept calling on the "funeral stopper." The next morning, the doctors took new X-rays and told them to keep up whatever they were doing, for things looked slightly better. Over the following days, Rich developed pneumonia and then a high fever; the doctors told his parents it would be over shortly. But they kept on talking to the Lord.

Twenty-eight days after the accident, Rich woke up. Medical science had no explanation for what happened. But he woke up. Therapy followed, but Rich was told to accept his limitations. He was, by this time, talking to the Lord himself. He asserted his faith that he would walk again. Not only did Rich walk again sixteen months after his wreck, but the boy all the doctors gave up on—the one who would not live through the night—finished the Boston Marathon, a footrace of more than twenty-six miles.[4]

Today, my question is not, "Who does Jesus think He is?" No, my question is, "Who do *you* think He is?"

---

4 https://sprenkel.com/story.html

The answer we give will determine our faith in His power. I hope you will see Him as the Almighty, able to deliver His people. Anything less casts a shadow across His wondrous power. May He show up in our lives as He did at that funeral.

SERMON OUTLINE

Introduction: This story, related only by Luke, is powerful. Some scholars want to doubt its authenticity because it is found only here. The question is, "How many times does God have to say something before it is divine?" The answer is a resounding, "Once!"

Jesus and His team neared Nain and encountered a funeral. Coming out of the city, this large gathering ran into the Son of Man. Suddenly, Jesus did the unthinkable. He stopped a funeral and touched a casket. He even started talking to a corpse. His actions, no doubt, caused people to start asking, "Who does He think He is?" In a few moments, they would discover the answer.

1. COMMON MAN
    a. One of Us
    b. One Among Us
    c. One Often Missed by Us
2. COMPASSIONATE MAN
    a. Shocking Statement
    b. Standing With the Weak
    c. Struggle on Our Part
3. CONQUERING MAN
    a. Simple Statement
    b. Sending a Thought
    c. Stretching Into the Future

Conclusion: Too many among us have given up on Jesus. He still thinks (and knows) He is the Lord of lords and the answer to our issues. God has come through Jesus to help His people, as Luke 7:16 declares.

STUDY QUESTIONS

1. Do we take Scripture seriously enough? Are there things God has spoken through His Word that we easily discard? What does His Word say about such action?
2. Does Jesus have permission in your life to upset social norms? How might His commands run contradictory to culturally accepted mores? Are you willing to stand out as one who follows His demands rather than those of our society?
3. Jesus was among the people, actually one of them. How does this image conflict with the images of religious figures today? How might we all become more like Him in this regard?
4. How does His role as your High Priest in Heaven (Hebrews 4:15-16) impact your life? What does eternity look like because of His role in this regard?
5. Have you ever been in a season where you overlooked His nearness? What helped you rediscover the closeness of the Father?
6. What does the Resurrection mean to you? How should we live with the day in our future approaching when Jesus will call every living soul who ever walked the earth back to life to stand before Him in judgment?

7

JOHN: A WONDERING MYSTERY

> Then the disciples of John reported to him concerning all these things. And John, calling two of his disciples to him, sent them to Jesus, saying, "Are You the Coming One, or do we look for another?" When the men had come to Him, they said, "John the Baptist has sent us to You, saying, 'Are You the Coming One, or do we look for another?'" And that very hour He cured many of infirmities, afflictions, and evil spirits; and to many blind He gave sight. Jesus answered and said to them, "Go and tell John the things you have seen and heard: that the blind see, the lame walk, the lepers are cleansed, the deaf hear, the dead are raised, the poor have the gospel preached to them. And blessed is he who is not offended because of Me" (Luke 7:18–23).

We have already encountered a cousin of Jesus. He is the great John the Baptist. What a man! Better yet, what a man of God. His story moves me deeply, challenges me, and makes me want to fall on my face before God and ask for mercy. At the same time, it brings great comfort by revealing a side of the man about whom Jesus said, "Among those born of women there has not risen one greater" (Matthew 11:11). His life speaks to my weaknesses—my inner struggles. Thankfully, his story also reveals the remedy for my issues.

Mistaken Ideas

This scene is a gathering of mistaken ideas—a concoction of unrealized expectations. John had been so adamant about the identity of Jesus, so emphatic in his declaration that this Jesus was indeed the Lamb of God who would take away the world's sin (John 1:29), that it is hard to witness his struggle. Still, that is precisely what we see. This should strike none of us as being strange, for the coming of the Son of God into the world had brought challenge and hardship into John's life.

When still in his mother's womb, the presence of the Lamb of God interrupted his pre-birth rest and caused him to leap for joy (Luke 1:41). Later, in preparation for the coming ministry of Jesus, he retreated from society and lived in the wilderness. His ministry demanded that he preach like a wild man, eat rough food, and wear clothing that was neither stylish nor comfortable (Matthew 3:4; 11:7-9). His flourishing ministry had been taken over by his cousin, leaving him virtually alone (John 3:26). Now, he sits in a filthy prison cell. In all probability, he has been locked away for about eighteen months. That is especially tough for an outdoorsman.

Faced with the mounting pressure and the never-ending derision of the enemy assaulting him day and night, John wonders if what he had preached was true. *Is it worth all I have given?* That had to be a question plaguing him as the monotony of prison life crept by.

Mortal After All

Some scholars disagree with my assessment of John. They assert various reasons why his messengers were sent and spin the questions so John does not appear to be wavering. It's as if they must hang a superhero cape across his weary shoulders. He must, in their estimation, become an aberration from the rest of humanity. I think they mean well by setting such a high standard, but in the end, they have created such a high bar that no one can ever hope to be used by God.

Do you want to know why John asked this question? It is simple. He was hurting, and he was not a superhero. He had been locked away in Herod's filthy prison for months, and no one appeared to be doing anything about it. None of the Jews to whom he had preached were protesting outside the palace, demanding his release. None of the Essenes, a religious group devoted to strict observance of a holy life, were setting up appointments with the political leaders in hopes of intervention. Worst of all, Jesus—the One he had declared with such vigor to be the Lamb of God, and the One who declared Himself to be anointed to *"set at liberty . . . the oppressed"* (Luke 4:18)—had not lifted a finger to get him released. Jesus had not even come to visit him!

No matter how tough you are, that would hurt. Jesus never darkened the door of John's prison cell. I contend John was human enough that it stung when he thought about Jesus not caring enough to enact his release. So, John did what the rest of us do when we find ourselves in that spot—he began to have questions about Jesus.

In *Will the Real Jesus Please Stand Up?* by William Craig and John Crossan, a debate takes place about the identity of Jesus. One viewpoint takes what you and I hold dear about Jesus and trashes it. The other defends what we believe with equal vigor. They search for the "real" Jesus through study, intellectualism, and research. They do their best to find Him by looking back through dusty history and then coming to the proper conclusion.

John, languishing in prison, did the same thing. His biggest issue was the "very real" Jesus was less than twenty miles from his prison cell and not doing what he thought the Messiah should be doing for him. Honestly, isn't that always the crux of our struggle? We think we know what Jesus should be doing, and He refuses to act according to our script.

Let's look closer at John. We think he was part of the aforementioned Essene party. They were a fiery group devoted to a godly national Israel. They wanted to see Jehovah elevated in the political, moral, and educational realms in Israel, somewhat like Moses had earlier established. They were as patriotic as anyone you will ever see wearing red, white, and blue in America. They were devoted to Jehovah, and John was a rising star in their establishment. And like them, John was looking for Jesus to swoop in and lead them to the ultimate victory. Only their version of victory hinged on casting out all things Roman and the elevation of all things Moses.

John wanted fire and judgment. He wanted to hear from his Messiah messages such as, "I am amassing a great army; we are going to march on the Roman headquarters next Tuesday! In a few weeks, the Romans will be gone, and sinners will be kicked out of town!" Instead, John was hearing things attributed to Jesus that were deeply troubling.

> "But I tell you not to resist an evil person. But whoever slaps you on your right cheek, turn the other to him also. If anyone wants to sue you and take away your tunic, let him have your cloak also. And whoever compels you to go one mile, go with him two. Give to him who asks you, and from him who wants to borrow from you do not turn away. You have heard that it was said, 'You shall love your neighbor and hate your enemy.' But I say to you, love your enemies, bless those who curse

> you, do good to those who hate you, and pray for those who spitefully use you and persecute you" (Matthew 5:39–44).

Those were not the pre-battle prep talks John was expecting. On top of that, Jesus was going about the countryside talking about—of all things—"eating and drinking" with "tax collectors and sinners!" (Matthew 11:19).

That had to be hard for someone like John to stomach. His cousin was talking about getting along with the Romans and hanging out with sinners, and John began wondering whether Jesus was really the answer. Also, John was now rotting in prison while Jesus seemed to be out having a great time, living life to the fullest, and John's muddled thinking becomes easier to understand. Simply stated, John was having a hard time because Jesus was not acting like John thought He should act. John's religion and Jesus' actions were not meshing, and John couldn't grasp what was going on.

Isn't that what we have endured? We have witnessed one Christian being healed but another die from the same disease. We have scratched our heads because a drunk person was spared in a wreck while their lack of caution caused a Christian's death. I have shrugged my shoulders in wonder when a godless and profane person made millions while a believer went bankrupt. I have wondered why a wonderful saint suffered greatly while a blatant sinner waltzed through life with "nary a scratch." I have never understood why I preached a funeral for a grizzled old sinner who lived to be 100 years old one week and did the same for a devoted couple's infant son who died of a rare cancer the next week. Like John, I have sometimes *wondered.*

To make matters worse, my blood boils when a religious wolf pops up and says there has to be something wrong with us because people with real faith do not endure such struggles. In other words, you are a second-class citizen if you struggle with issues. You are less than ideal if you wonder about the hardships of life. Here's what I have discovered about the preachers on that circuit: They never stick around after the things they have so glibly promised fall through. They are off to the next crowd, pockets bulging with cash, promising a religious Jesus who is always "Johnny on the spot," the panacea for every ill and hurt.

The next time one of them levels a charge because you are struggling with issues, ignore them and remember John. He was, at one time, on top of the religious world. He was the leading evangelist of the day. He had the biggest crowds and the largest following before Jesus came along. On top of that, he was now in prison, and it seemed like Jesus did not care at all. He wondered if Jesus was who He claimed to be. Yet Jesus stated this wondering man was the greatest prophet ever to grace our planet.

Let's face the truth about Jesus. Not the make-believe Jesus touted in American "churchianity." Not the conjured-up Jesus portrayed on stage shows. No, we must encounter the real Jesus—the New Testament Jesus.

When we set aside the fanciful, make-believe Messiah, we will find strong medicine. It is not milk for babes; it is meat for men and women. This is gritty, salty, where-we-live truth. The real Jesus may have in mind for you to live a life so financially blessed that it surpasses your wildest dreams. Then again, He might have in His plan for you to sell every vestige of wealth and invest it all in world missions. This real Jesus, not the cartoon character put forth by many today, may have in mind for you to live to a ripe old age, having never experienced as much as a headache. Of course, if you fall ill and suffer greatly before meeting Him in Heaven, it might be His intention as well. Why such different lots in life? Don't ask me, for I have no idea. Jesus may allow you to roll through life with someone calling you a disparaging name like "holy roller" or "Charis-maniac" as the worst thing that will happen to you. Or, His plan may include laying down your life as a martyr.

Message Sent

What happens when we are no longer riding the high tide of public adulation and instead are locked away in prison? How do we handle it when things turn from blessing to blasting? What do we do when Jesus knows we are struggling, and it seems He is keeping His distance?

If you are struggling, fighting, or trying to keep your head above water today, listen closely to the message Jesus sent to John: *"Blessed is he who is not offended because of Me"* (Luke 7:23). On the surface, that response seems so callous and unfeeling it is hard to attribute it to Jesus. Then I stop and remember I am meeting the real Jesus, not the stick figure most people hear about today.

I tremble when I stop to think about what Jesus *did not* do. He never tried to apologize to John or smooth things over with him. His message is unlike anything we hear from the church-growth gurus today. Amazingly, Jesus never tried to explain Himself. He did not promise to do better. He did not say He would change one thing. He based His life on truth. Even when truth was a bitter pill, Jesus stood there unmoved.

If what Jesus *did not* do is alarming, what He *did* is amazing. When the messengers asked the question John sent to the Lord, He basically told them to stand aside and watch a while. He then did two things. First, He demonstrated His immense power by healing people with afflictions. The passage implies contact—possibly an allusion to diseases such as leprosy fleeing from His personal touch.

Not only did He miraculously cure sicknesses and diseases, but He also cast out devils. Luke's differentiation of these two stunning acts should let us know that not all sickness is associated with demonic intervention, or there would have been no distinction made. He gave sight to a large number of blind people, freeing them from the bondage of their individual darkness (Luke 7:21). What a display to behold! It was almost as if Jesus, after telling them to sit down and watch, assaulted every debilitating situation in sight. The messengers from John's prison cell had to be stupefied by what they witnessed.

After shredding every opposing force within range, Jesus turned to address the messengers. I am sure they were ready for a statement to take back to John unlike anything they dreamed possible. After witnessing an hour of power, they were tingling with excitement. They were ready to hear, "You guys go tell My cousin what you just saw. In fact, you tell him I am on My way down there tomorrow, and just like I have freed all these people from their personal prisons, I am going to blast him out of jail."

That, shockingly, was not what Jesus said to the wide-eyed emissaries. Instead, He told them, "Tell John I am performing My mission. Don't get offended and lose sight of that." That's it? I can almost hear one of them saying, "You want us to go back to the greatest prophet ever and tell him you are too busy doing your work to come and get him out of jail?"

As difficult as it was to hear, Jesus was doing what He was sent to do. That is precisely the point some of us have reached in our journey with Him. Are we willing to trust a Jesus who does something for someone else but not for us? Can we hold on to Him when, in His mission, He calls on us for sacrifice?

We need to be reminded that John the Baptist died in that nasty prison while Simon Peter walked out due to divine intervention. Recall that James was beheaded while John lived to be an old man.

I believe the greatest display of faith is not when something supernatural is publicly displayed. It is not when a man lays hands on the sick, and they are healed. It is not when a woman hears from God and speaks a prophetic word that rings true. In my estimation, the greatest feat of faith is when Jesus demands something tough from us, and we, sometimes wondering, say, "Lord, let it be unto me according to Your word."[1]

Those who are truly happy—the Bible calls them "blessed"—are the ones who do not walk away when the path gets hard.[2] In particular, the blessed refuse to walk away even when they observe others who have a relatively easy journey while they struggle. They willingly embrace the cross before them and believe God controls their lives. They are fully committed to the outworking that is "pleasing in His sight" (Hebrews 13:21). "His will be done" is their marching song.

We have a choice to make. Some among us desperately need to come to Jesus and fall before Him as the Savior. Not the savior of the pablum-filled gospel so prevalent today. Instead, the call is for those who are so desperate, so intent on finding Him, it matters not what He calls us to do. No sacrifice is too great. No demand is too taxing. No cost is too severe. As long as He works out His mission in our lives, it always ends well.

The call is for young men and women who, at the beginning of their prime years, will take seriously the call that falls from

---

[1] Mary said this very thing in Luke 1:38. Hardship would accompany her surrender.

[2] Matthew 5:3-10 puts on display the spirit of commitment in the face of hardship.

His lips, "Take up [your] cross and follow Me!" (Matthew 16:24). The call is for mothers and fathers, settled into the ruts of life, to once again take a long and pondering look at where they stand with the One who called for the ultimate sacrifice from the greatest prophet who ever lived. Are you ready for such an adventure? If you are a senior adult, He has more in store for you than growing old and tired as you spend your monthly retirement check. There is a call for senior saints who have trod the path before us to rise in fire and devotion and blaze a new trail—lit with the passion and anointing of the Holy Spirit as He calls us to follow hard on your heels, straight into the battle and ultimately into eternal rewards.

Yes, John had his moment. He was that much like me. However, I am convinced the moment after the axe hit his neck, every wondering question was erased as the One who did not come to see him in prison met him with open arms. John's questions were answered clearly when Jesus welcomed a completely whole and healed cousin into His everlasting kingdom. The day will come when we meet a man in eternity who wondered but won. May we follow in his footsteps.

SERMON OUTLINE

Introduction: We have already met John the Baptist, a cousin of the Master. What a man! Better, what a man of God. His story, particularly this vignette, makes me want to fall on my face before our Lord and ask for mercy. At the same time, it reveals to me a side of the one Jesus called "the greatest prophet ever to live" which is seldom put on display. Thankfully, it also presents us with the remedy for our own wondering moments.

1. MISTAKEN IDEAS
   a. Assured of His Identity
   b. Accepting Hardships
   c. Asking Tough Questions
2. MORTAL AFTER ALL
   a. Struggling with Self
   b. Searching for the Real Jesus
   c. Strong Medicine
3. MESSAGE SENT
   a. A Changing Tide
   b. A Challenging Demand
   c. Confronting the Enemy

Conclusion: Those who are genuinely happy are the ones who wonder but wait on God for His timing and answer. John had his moment of wonder but won.May we walk in his footsteps.

Study Questions

1. John suffered from unrealized expectations. Have you ever been in the same position in your walk with God? How have you dealt with your disappointment?
2. Can the real Jesus ever be discovered apart from faith? If not, why not?
3. In light of all we hear about Jesus, what do you think is His relationship between Himself and the sinner?
4. How do you handle the seeming contradictions in life? Consider the words of the psalmist (Psalm 73). How did he come to grips with his quandary about the apparent inequities in God's ways?
5. Has Jesus made a challenging demand in your life? Are you surrendered to His call?
6. How is the Kingdom demonstrated today? Are you taking part in the advancement of God's kingdom? How might you become involved?
7. Discuss the impact of an eternity with Jesus as motivation to fully surrender to God. Does anything we endure here compare to what awaits us there?

8

A TALE OF TWO RESPONSES

Then He began to rebuke the cities in which most of His mighty works had been done, because they did not repent: "Woe to you, Chorazin! Woe to you, Bethsaida! For if the mighty works which were done in you had been done in Tyre and Sidon, they would have repented long ago in sackcloth and ashes. But I say to you, it will be more tolerable for Tyre and Sidon in the day of judgment than for you. And you, Capernaum, who are exalted to heaven, will be brought down to Hades; for if the mighty works which were done in you had been done in Sodom, it would have remained until this day. But I say to you that it shall be more tolerable for the land of Sodom in the day of judgment than for you." At that time Jesus answered and said, "I thank You, Father, Lord of heaven and earth, that You have hidden these things from the wise and prudent and have revealed them to babes. Even so, Father, for so it seemed good in Your sight. All things have been delivered to Me by My Father, and no one knows the Son except the Father. Nor does anyone know the Father except the Son, and the one to whom the Son wills to reveal Him. Come to Me, all you who labor and are heavy laden, and I will give you rest. Take My yoke upon you and learn from Me, for I am gentle and lowly in heart, and you will find rest for

> your souls. For My yoke is easy and My burden is light" (Matthew 11:20-30).

We come now to a rather odd text. We are bypassing the narrative centering on John the Baptist, as we have already examined him and his relationship with Jesus. Instead, we reach a major turning point in the ministry of Jesus. Rejection of His ministry had been growing among the religious leaders and reached an impasse. It was now clear His life was headed to condemnation and death. The rejection by many in Israel was settled in bedrock. Before long, the path chosen by the religious leaders would not only be the choice of the overwhelming majority, but it would also be irreversible and finalized by Pilate.

Luke sets this scene in conjunction with the sending of the Seventy on a ministry tour. For our purposes, we are going to take the narrative as Matthew records it. This is a story of two responses. Before us are two choices regarding Jesus. Either we embrace Him and take upon our lives the yoke of His lordship, or we reject Him and invite the judgment that follows. There is no middle ground or placing Him on the back burner until we make up our minds. No, there is only here and now. The choice falls to each of us whether or not we are going to make Him the center of our lives.

A Dark, Foreboding Warning

The lips of Jesus here seem totally out of character, at least in the eyes of many people. If you see Jesus as nothing more than a candy-coated guy who always gives in and lets everyone have their way, then the image of the Lord here will surprise you. It might even be a shocking revelation about the true nature of Christ.

It's as if a dark and somber mood came over Jesus. He moved from the accusations of the religious leaders to a prophetic voice of judgment. In a scorching denunciation of two nearby cities, Jesus dredged up images of hellfire and brimstone that would put any modern preacher to shame: *"But I say to you that it shall be more tolerable for the land of Sodom in the day of judgment than for you"* (Matthew 11:24).

These two towns, Chorazin and Bethsaida, were suburbs of Capernaum, the home base for Jesus' ministry while in Galilee. There were three to four miles of distance between these hamlets. This area had been blessed, occupying front-row seats to many stunning works of Jesus:

- Healing a nobleman's son
- Healing a paralytic
- Casting out a demon in the synagogue
- Healing Peter's mother-in-law
- Healing a centurion's servant
- The raising of Jairus' daughter from the dead
- Healing of the woman with the issue of blood.

Who knows the true number of astounding things this area witnessed as Jesus invaded the domain of Satan? The miracle power Jesus displayed attracted large crowds. Yet, Jesus wasn't interested in large crowds for the sake of numbers. He longed for repentance in the onlookers' lives. Miracles were not a sideshow to Him. They were a validation of His ministry and message.[1]

Amazingly, despite all they had seen, few people accepted Him as Lord and Messiah. Regardless of what they had witnessed and felt, they chose to walk away and harden their hearts to Him.

[1] In his Gospel, John indicates miraculous works were "signs" pointing people to the divinity of Jesus (2:11, 18, 23; 3:2; 4:54; 6:2; 9:16; 11:47; 12:18, 37; 20:30).

All the goodness and grace shown by the Father in sending the Messiah into their midst was tossed aside like a dirty towel. They threw it all back in His face and rejected Him outright!

I am afraid this speaks to us more than we like to admit. How much of His mercy and grace has He poured into us? How many times has He kept us alive when we should have died? How often has He cooed to us like a dove, but we walked away from Him cold and indifferent? How many Sundays has He pleaded with us to surrender and make Him absolute Lord, only to have us walk out of church like nothing of consequence took place? How many times has He called and pleaded to let Him break the sin that holds us fast, only for us to shrug Him off? How often has He called to His church—standing outside, knocking, begging to get in and have fellowship—only to be left out in the cold like some unwanted stranger?

Oh yes, we have been the recipient of more blessings, greater grace, and larger opportunity than any generation in the history of the world. We have more technology, comfort, training, buildings, influence in government, money, and more of everything we say we need to reach the world and live in victory. Yet, the church in America has come to a virtual halt!

A Dangerous Time Lies Ahead

Jesus plainly said those afforded greater opportunity will face a greater day of reckoning. He compared those who now reject His grace to those who had already faced judgment.

He mentioned Tyre and Sidon—two cities from the past. God destroyed these Phoenician towns because of their extreme wickedness and the oppression of His people. Tyre fell to Alexander the Great in 332 BC, while Sidon was sacked by the Assyrians in 67 BC. In an interesting twist, Jesus said if those towns had witnessed the mighty works the inhabitants of Galilee had seen, they would have fallen on their faces in sackcloth and ashes. They would have humbled themselves to the dust in repentance.

When faced with such heavy words and somber prospects, should we not fall on our faces in repentance and brokenness before the Lord? Considering how much God has blessed us, should we not tremble in awe at His majesty? I think we all would agree that is appropriate.

Why, then, do we flippantly come and go from His presence, unchanged, unmoved, and unaltered in our ways? When we have been the recipients of grace and love, heard the message over and over, and sensed the nearness of His presence, how can we be unmoved about our standing with such a holy God?

I fear lest we blindly walk into the judgment of God. Like those in Chorazin and Bethsaida who witnessed His goodness, enjoyed the entertainment around Him, and marveled at what He could do in others but never bowed before Him as Lord, I tremble at the prospect of His impending judgment. I urge you (and I include myself in this appeal) to stop being a spectator, watching to see what God might do in the life of someone else, and instead bow in humble submission to Him. Quit worrying about how someone else responds to the movement of His Spirit and move close to Him yourself. Cease in your worry over the relationship someone else has with the Lord, and make sure you have surrendered in your heart.

Judgment Does Come!

Here is some alarming news: His judgment will come. It did to the ancient cities Jesus mentioned, and it did to the two cities He rebuked. In a similar fashion, it will come to those who knowingly walk away from His tender love and care. In fact, the judgment we will face if we reject Him will be worse than for someone who never knew the Lord. If you don't believe me, pay attention to these haunting words from Hebrews 10:28-31:

> Anyone who has rejected Moses' law dies without mercy on the testimony of two or three witnesses. Of how much worse punishment, do you suppose, will he be thought worthy who has trampled the Son of God underfoot, counted the blood of the covenant by which he was sanctified a common thing, and insulted the Spirit of grace? For we know Him who said, "Vengeance is Mine, I will repay," says the Lord. And again, "The Lord will judge His people." It is a fearful thing to fall into the hands of the living God.

Under the law of Moses, two to three witnesses were required to convict someone of blasphemy. The penalty was swift and sure death, usually by stoning. There was no mercy, no court of appeal, and no recourse. The Holy Spirit multiplied that by telling us a far greater judgment will come to all who trample Christ's blood underfoot, insulting "the Spirit of grace."

Also, we shouldn't think this applies only to the unsaved and not us. Verse 30 clearly says, *"The Lord will judge His people."* This is talking about those who know the Lord but flaunt their will and purpose over His, refusing to surrender to Him. This is not addressed to those who are unsaved and dead in sin. This is referring to those who harbor sin, cover it up, and nurse it, all the while knowing He calls us to forsake our sin and lead a holy life for Him. It's a fearful thing to do that and face God.

The thought makes me cry, "Oh God, purge me of my sin! Make me clean in Your sight." I feel like the psalmist David, a man all too aware of personal failure, who wrote: *"Search me, O God, and know my heart; try me, and know my anxieties;*

and see if there is any wicked way in me, and lead me in the way everlasting" (Psalm 139:23-24).

I want God to find the "wicked way" in my life and root it out so I can walk in the everlasting ways of His blessing. The last thing I want is to spend my life in church studying and singing about Him but never bowing in total submission to Him. The results of that choice are too horrible to imagine.

A Deliberate Choice

There is another choice we can make. It carries such a blessed result that it's a wonder the whole world doesn't respond by rushing into Christ's presence. Jesus shifted from a pounding condemnation to a peaceful call:

> "Come to Me, all you who labor and are heavy laden, and I will give you rest. Take My yoke upon you and learn from Me, for I am gentle and lowly in heart, and you will find rest for your souls. For My yoke is easy and My burden is light" (Matthew 11:28-30).

April 3, 1974, is a signal date in my life. It was a Wednesday, and that night, I tried to preach my first sermon. I was a boy preacher who felt an urgent call and did my best to answer. I took Matthew 11:28-30 as my text and stumbled through in an attempt to preach. Not only did I not do it justice then, but I still never have. The reason? It is humanly impossible to describe this sublime call given by the Son of God in a few words. What Jesus said shouts for our attention. Coming fast on the heels of a staggering warning, the Lord calls to any and all to fall before Him. In the place of heavy judgment, He offers joy and peace unlike anything found on earth.

Jesus gives us a simple plan of how to get into the presence of God. It's not hard, complex, or hidden from view.

Jesus is unlike some preachers and teachers who make getting into the presence of God sound so detailed and difficult that you need an advanced Ivy League degree to reach Him. They have their formulas and catchwords, and many have a price tag attached. They will, for a fee, help you find the presence of God.

That is not how Jesus does business. He's simple, even too simple for some. But He knows how to get there! If your goal is to get into the presence of the Almighty, follow Jesus' simple plan, and you can get there in a moment!

First, Realize Your Need

Jesus addressed all those who labor and are loaded down. He's talking about people who know they have a problem. They are also aware they can't handle it on their own. That is always the first step in getting to God—realizing your need and that you can't get help elsewhere. Only when you come to God in repentance and confession will you be forgiven (1 John 1:9). You will never get healed until you admit you are sick and then come to the Lord.[2] You will never be baptized in the Holy Spirit until you realize the lack in your life and decide to receive this blessing from the Father.[3] No church will ever have revival until realizing its need and then calling on God (see Revelation 3:14-21). Herein lies the wonderful, glorious truth from Jesus: Whatever it may be, everyone who dares to realize their need is welcome!

I love the word *all.* It's so powerful and complete. *All* is so vast that it includes the person who has drifted from God for decades. *All* is so exhaustive that it includes the one who harbors great sin kept hidden from everyone.

---

[2] It falls on the sick person to call for the elders to pray for him rather than the church seeking out the sick person (James 5:14).
[3] Christ gives the Spirit to those who obey Him (Acts 5:32).

All is so broad that it encompasses those who have given up on ever seeing victory. *All* is so wide that it includes those whom the town uses as fodder for gossip and whom the church has decided are no longer worth the effort to reach. If you can find anyone who falls outside the word *all*, you have found one who is beyond Jesus' touch. Glorious is the thought that "none" are outside "all"!

Second, Come to Jesus

Move. Get up and make the trip. Christ's glorious invitation is a lighthouse shining in the darkness of our sin.

Throughout history, people have sought a way to get God's attention. The ancient Jews were taught to keep the Law. The pagans created systems to catch the eye of some false deity. Men today will walk through hot coals, crawl like serpents over great distances, and make horrible sacrifices. Women will do unspeakable things like throw their babies into rivers to be devoured by crocodiles. It is all done to catch the eye of some pagan god. Meanwhile, the Creator of the universe stands before us and says, "Come."

I am puzzled at our hesitancy to get up and go. Why do we resist running into His loving arms? What keeps us from pushing forward to get into His presence?

You will have to make the effort to come to Him. Sure, He will call to you, woo you, draw you, and even plead with you to make the short trip into His presence. But you will still have to come. Don't take my word for it. Consider this passage:

> Then He saw them straining at rowing, for the wind was against them. Now about the fourth watch of the night He came to them, walking on the sea, and would have passed them by. And when they saw

> Him walking on the sea, they supposed it was a ghost, and cried out; for they all saw Him and were troubled. But immediately He talked with them and said to them, "Be of good cheer! It is I; do not be afraid." Then He went up into the boat to them, and the wind ceased. And they were greatly amazed in themselves beyond measure, and marveled (Mark 6:48-51).

Jesus was going to walk past the struggling disciples: *"He would have passed them by."* Had they not called out to Him, they would have spent the rest of that night struggling. Jesus would walk right past them in the middle of their great struggle. Things are no different today. Jesus has made the trip through the stormy seas of time and space, and now we must call out to Him. He has even ventured into the room you now occupy, but you must make the move that brings the two of you together.

For some of us, coming to Him means humility. It means breaking through our pride and acknowledging our way hasn't worked. For some of us, coming to Him means repentance. It means we are ready to forsake our sins and come clean before Him. For others, coming to Him means taking the risk that He will meet us. We must use faith to believe what we cannot sense. Coming to Him might mean admitting we have been wrong—we don't have it all together. But what awaits us in His presence is worth any sacrifice to make the trip. Do what we must; we must come before Him today!

Relinquish Everything to Jesus

It is here that things become difficult. It's where many drop out. To get into His presence, we must surrender. Taking His yoke upon us means we are willing to submit to His direction in our lives.

Know this: Everyone here will wear some type of yoke for the rest of their life. Everyone. For some, it's a yoke of pride—a heavy and lonesome yoke once it has become well-worn. It could be a yoke of addiction—an oppressive burden to bear. Another yoke is bitterness—a gruesome weight that makes us and everyone around us miserable. For some, it's a yoke of materialism—a ponderous chain that grows larger the longer we allow it to bind us. It might be a yoke of failure as we allow our mistakes to weigh us down every day. There are millions of yokes worn by humanity. Broken marriages, mistakes made with our children, bad career decisions, hidden sins we don't want anyone to discover, and financial mistakes we are still paying for years later—the list is endless.

Today, right now, the divine Helper calls out for us to come to Him and to allow Him to take off the yokes of our own making and replace them with the One of His choosing. Sure, we still wear a yoke. But His yoke is easy. Yes, we are still in servitude. But look at the difference. The yokes of our making are large, chafing, heavy, debilitating, and grueling. But His yoke is light, bearable, joyful, and glorious.

Yes, I bear His yoke. But when all is said and done, I shall not be cast aside like some worn-out old ox, no longer capable of bearing the load. Instead, I will be ushered into His glorious presence where I will hear a "well done" from His gracious lips. I am a servant in His Kingdom. Yet I will one day wear a crown in His glorious presence.

How will you respond to Him today? As for me, I plan on heeding His call to "come" into His presence and receive His fresh touch.

SERMON OUTLINE

Introduction: This text contradicts the idea that Jesus has nothing to do with judgment. This passage will make some uncomfortable with their image of the Master. It is far better now to encounter truth and make the right response than to wait until it is too late to hear and come to the Master.

1. A DARK WARNING
   a. Shocking Revelation
   b. Somber Renunciation
   c. Sad Realization
2. A DANGEROUS TIME AHEAD
   a. Ancient History
   b. Appropriate Action
   c. Alarming News
3. A DELIBERATE CHOICE
   a. Realize Your Need
   b. Respond to the Call
   c. Relinquish All

Conclusion: You will still wear a yoke, but the burden will be much easier. You will still be a servant, but the Master will be gracious. In the end, the response you make will determine the reward you reap.

STUDY QUESTIONS

1. How do these straightforward words of Jesus make you feel? Does anything He said here contradict your opinions of the Master?

2. How can anything be worse than what happened to Sodom and Gomorrah (Genesis 19:24-25)? Read Psalm 9:17. Can you imagine the wrath of God stored up for our nation?
3. List acts of God's grace and mercy you have witnessed in our land. Do you see any parallels between the cities mentioned by Jesus and our nation?
4. Why do people tend to make entering God's presence difficult?
5. Do you realize your need for God? How have you responded to that realization?
6. Is anyone not a part of "all"? Why does this matter?
7. Is something standing between you and Jesus that you must relinquish? Is it really worth the threat of judgment?

9

HE SAID, SHE SAID

> Then one of the Pharisees asked Him to eat with him. And He went to the Pharisee's house, and sat down to eat. And behold, a woman in the city who was a sinner, when she knew that Jesus sat at the table in the Pharisee's house, brought an alabaster flask of fragrant oil, and stood at His feet behind Him weeping; and she began to wash His feet with her tears, and wiped them with the hair of her head; and she kissed His feet and anointed them with the fragrant oil. Now when the Pharisee who had invited Him saw this, he spoke to himself, saying, "This Man, if He were a prophet, would know who and what manner of woman this is who is touching Him, for she is a sinner" (Luke 7:36-39).

Jesus came to a banquet meal hosted by a Pharisee called Simon, where some astounding truths about Him were revealed. There are some striking similarities between this event and one described in the other Gospels, namely in Matthew 26, Mark 14, and John 12. However, there are some differences to be noted in the two events. There are different locations: one in the house of a Pharisee, the other in the house of a leper. In this account, only the feet of Jesus are anointed; in the other accounts, His head is anointed as well. The tears, prominent in Luke's account, are absent in the other readings. Luke's account takes place in the middle of Christ's Galilean ministry, while the others take place the week before His crucifixion.

Two different lessons are taught. Here, it is about the power of Christ to change a life and to give a second chance. In the other accounts, the greed of Judas as well as the example of spending money on the work of God are central.

When looking at the differences, I believe these were two separate events where Jesus was anointed. After all, isn't He worthy of praise many times over? Remember that we are given a limited number of glimpses into Jesus' life.

A Dinner Gathering

Have you ever dealt with an issue where you didn't know the whole story, perhaps something akin to helping a fractured marriage survive? One thing you go through is the "he said, she said" issue. You listen to both partners and try to learn as much as possible from how they act and what they say. This process can lead to some startling revelations.

Let's take this approach here. Basically, two characters revolve around the central guest, Jesus. Let's watch closely as both characters interact with the Master. He's the lightning rod, the VIP of the evening. Around Him are two individuals who act out a drama more powerful than anything you will ever watch on a screen or stage.

A Pharisee named Simon had invited Jesus to dinner. These dinners were lavish affairs, and the crowds gathering around would sometimes be large. Since Jesus was the guest of honor, the crowd outside the dining area was likely larger than the crowd inside.

The guests would have been seated around a short table with their feet and legs arranged under them and sticking out behind them. Had you been an onlooker, you would have seen a bunch of backs and the soles of feet. That's how they arranged for guests to dine. People would gather around the edges, eavesdrop as much as possible, and hopefully get a few scraps of the luxurious food. They could become part of whatever was happening at the table.

A Party Crasher

From the pressing crowd, a woman suddenly appeared behind the Master. According to the text, she was an immoral woman, most likely a prostitute. Some people wrongly believe this was Mary Magdalene, a woman Christ delivered from multiple demons. However, we don't know this woman's name. What matters is who she was when she walked up to Him and who she was when she walked away.

I love her story. It's so full of truth and laden with golden nuggets of hope that it's hard to exhaust them all in a few lines. What a trail she blazed for all of us who are in desperate need of the presence of the Lord! Perhaps earlier that day, Jesus had issued this wonderful invitation: *"Come to Me, all you who labor and are heavily laden, and I will give you rest. Take My yoke upon you and learn from Me, for I am gentle and lowly in heart, and you will find rest for your souls. For My yoke is easy and My burden is light"* (Matthew 11:28-30).

This woman decided to take Him up on His offer and go to His side despite how she had lived. Her immoral actions had broken the heart of God and likely many of the wives in that town. Her trade was ancient and equally lowly and detested. This was not some young girl who was caught smoking in the girls' restroom at school or cheating on an exam. She was considered as bad a sinner as one could be. Even Jesus used a double expression to describe her sins— admitting they were great and numerous. She would have been viewed as a slave of Satan. Bursting into Simon's party was a woman everyone viewed as bound, mean, tough, and hard.

Yet she left Jesus' presence changed. This desperate woman, who had no one on her side and no future, found a way to get directly into the presence of God's Son. I find hope here because Jesus didn't shove her aside or ask her to be removed. He didn't express revulsion or disgust. Instead, He let her into His presence. If He would let her touch Him—the ugly reaching out to the gracious, the stained touching the pure, the rejected grasping the One everyone clamored to be near—surely, He will let me touch Him as well.

There is hope for us. There is hope today that any and all who desire to come into His presence will be granted that request. The worst, the meanest, and the ones with the most soiled and ruined reputations can come into His presence and be touched by His mighty hand.

This woman's effusive act of worship has been studied, analyzed, and preached countless times. The bottom line is simple: Christ's grace had touched her, and she was not ashamed to demonstrate her gratitude. Her response was marked by brokenness. Perhaps it was conviction over sin or the joy of being forgiven. Maybe it was a combination of both. But she was broken before the Lord.

Weeping profusely, her tears began to soak Jesus' feet. Where nails would one day rip Jesus' flesh, her tears washed away the road's grime. Where blood will one day congeal and form ugly clots, the expensive oil from her bottle anointed His feet. When the puddle began to spill onto the dirty floor, she took down her hair and used it as a makeshift towel.

Her worship was powerful and unmistakable. For a woman to let her hair down in public was considered a disgrace, even a divorceable event. But this woman was not concerned with public propriety. The attitudes of the people around her did not matter. All that mattered was the gracious One before her who had changed her life forever.

Why did she act like she did? In discussing her actions with Simon the host, Jesus told a parable:

> "There was a certain creditor who had two debtors. One owed five hundred denarii, and the other fifty. And when they had nothing with which to repay, he freely forgave them both. Tell Me, therefore, which of them will love him more?" Simon answered and said, "I suppose the one whom he forgave more." And He said to him, "You have rightly judged" (Luke 7:41-43).

In this story, there was a creditor: a man who loaned out money. He had two clients; one owed him five hundred denarii, and the other owed him fifty. *Denarii* was a Roman term for what a common laborer would make in a day. For instance, if a laborer earned $20 an hour today, that would make a denarii worth about $160. For the sake of our story, let's use that amount.

Jesus presents a man who owed a creditor $8,000. The other guy owed about $80,000. In an amazing display of grace, the creditor called both guys up and said he was forgiving their debts. What a day that must have been for those two men!

Then Jesus asked a simple question: "Of those two, who do you think will like the creditor more?" Simon said, "The one who owed $80,000." Jesus congratulated him on getting that one right.

This woman acted like she did and expressed her hallelujah because she was an eighty-thousand-dollar sinner! She knew she had broken God's heart. She was aware she had distanced herself from God's will. She knew she was lost and undone, and she knew how far Jesus had to go to set her free.

Until you and I fully understand the message of verse 42—*"they had nothing with which to repay"*— our lives will remain distant, cold, and unaffected by any move of God. Until we realize we have no means to repay the Lord, we will be offended by another person's worship. We will remain aloof and arrogant. Our lives will be marked by pride in who we are and what we have accomplished. The tragedy of such a lifestyle forever removes any chance of us living in the presence of God, either here or in eternity. If one thing is clear, it is this: God will not allow carnal boasting in His presence (see 1 Corinthians 1:29).

That's why I pray for godly conviction to come into my life and church. Great preachers and teachers can stand before us all day and eloquently talk about sin. They can rail against pride, arrogance, haughtiness, lack of worship, coldness of heart, and on and on. However, until the Holy Ghost convicts us of our indifference and the desperate need we have for Christ, those words will fall flat or be sent back in rebellion.

The grasp of worship and the true meaning of abandonment in praise will never enter your spirit until you finally realize how lost you are and how far Christ had to go for you. You will never "get" passionate worship until it dawns deep in your heart how wicked you are apart from Him.

The reason I worship Him by "letting my hair down in public" and suffering the ridicule of many in the church world is because I know what I am apart from Christ. I know how damningly dark my heart is apart from the light He shines in my life. I grasp where I would be without His intervention in my life. So, I will worship and praise Him! If those at the table misunderstand me, so be it!

This woman demonstrated great *chutzpah*, which means she had a lot of nerve and gall. I love the hope she reveals, and I share in the hallelujah she gave Jesus. But I greatly admire her chutzpah—her determination.

Nobody had called her and asked, "Why don't you come over and eat with us? By the way, Jesus is going to be there." No, she wasn't invited. A close examination of the record will reveal that[1]. She wasn't on the guest list. However, she made up her mind once she discovered Jesus would be there.

Can you imagine the buzz of the crowd around her? "What's she doing here? Who does she think she is? How dare someone like her show up at something like this? Can you believe the nerve? If I had her reputation, there is no way I would darken the door!"

She never let it stop her. She was unfazed by the salacious gossip. The naysayers didn't hinder her for one moment. She had grit, and she was going to get close to the Master. Since Simon didn't invite her, she crashed the party.

How that speaks to today's church! We are so sensitive that we get bent out of shape if someone sits in "our" seat. We can't make it to church if rain is in the forecast. We get upset and leave the church if someone doesn't pat us on the back or speak to us. We get mad if someone doesn't say the right thing about us.

We need to find some of the chutzpah she displayed—an attitude that screams, "I don't care what you say about me!" It's time some of us get over how we are treated in the foyer and worry more about meeting the Master at the altar. Having the right people shake our hands or hug our necks is secondary

---

[1] Luke 7:37 reveals she heard about Him being at the dinner. She was not invited, but rather heard the buzz of gossip about the Master being at the meal.

to the touch of Christ's hand or His embrace. We must develop such chutzpah that we don't care if others laugh, condemn, talk about, or make fun of us. All that matters is that we get to Jesus.

You must press in where you can touch the Master. Any effort expended will be well rewarded. It doesn't matter if you must fight through a crowd like the woman with a hemorrhaging disease (Matthew 9:20-22). The fact that you are not as tall as everyone else is irrelevant. That was one of the issues with Zacchaeus, but he fought through his limitations by climbing a tree to get close to the Master (Luke 19:1-10). Don't let inconvenience stop you. Keep crying out like blind Bartimaeus (Mark 10:46-52). You may have to scream for help like the disciples on a stormy sea (Mark 6:48) or grovel at His feet like a hopeless Gentile woman (Matthew 15:22).

All that matters is those who dare to press in and do not care what others say about them are met by the One able to do amazing things. Everyone at that night's dinner scorned this unnamed woman because of her sin. Yet the only sinless one in the crowd welcomed her and changed her life forever. Press in, my friend. Fight on, my brother. Struggle on, my companion in the battle. What awaits when you finally touch Him will be worth any burden you must bear!

A Disgruntled Governor

Our attention shifts to the governor of the feast, Simon. It is time to endure the "he said" part of the story. It's not as lengthy because there isn't much good to be said about this guy and his response. I know Simon invited Jesus to his house, but he wasn't having Jesus over to dinner; he wanted to *have* Jesus for dinner.

Simon brought Jesus to his house to put Him to the test, to see what He was made of. In the end, Simon was placed on the examination table and found wanting on many levels. He knew all about the Old Testament law, theology, ethics, ceremonial purity, and temple worship. He excelled in everything a good Pharisee would know. But he made a failing grade on the exam that mattered most. To add insult to injury, an immoral woman who knew little about God wound up passing with flying colors. When it comes to this business of the Kingdom, you never know.

Simon made a couple of terrible mistakes. Many of us commit these same errors despite knowing this story.

First, he compared himself to the woman and mistakenly thought because his sin wasn't as bad as hers, he was in the clear. Honestly, isn't there just a bit of this in all of us? Are we not all prone to saying, or at least thinking, "I would never do what they have done"? I have heard such thinking all my life. In my earlier ignorance, I made the same type of arrogant boast. Thankfully, time and experience have tempered my zeal in that arena.

The problem is when we say, "I would never do that!" with self-exaltation in our voice. There's a bubbling up of pride—a concealed air of snobbishness. We secretly cherish a bit of smug glee when we realize there are people who have committed sins more heinous than our paltry failures.

You may take pride in knowing you have never been drunk, spaced out on drugs, committed adultery, or robbed a bank. Great! Rejoice that you are not an eighty-thousand-dollar sinner. But if you think for one moment you are not an eighty-thousand-dollar sinner, think again. It doesn't matter if you are only an eight-dollar sinner, you are in the same boat with the rest of us. You can't pay back what you owe, and if Someone hadn't paid the price for you, you'd wind up in hell with all of us eighty-thousand dollar people. So, in the end, nobody has anything to brag about because nobody has any great standard in their lives by which everyone else is to be measured.[2]

Second, Simon mistakenly thought his opinion of the woman and that of Jesus were the same. He followed an A + B = C line of logic:

A. If Jesus were really a prophet, He would know what kind of woman was touching Him.

B. If He knew, He would not allow her near Him.

C. Therefore, Jesus must not be a prophet.

Simon took his measuring stick—his limited knowledge of God—and since Jesus wasn't acting like he thought God should act, Jesus couldn't be the Messiah. The fault in his logic lay in point B. Simon was mistaken about Jesus. Not only did Jesus know what kind of woman she was, but He was more than willing to let her into His presence so she might be changed. The host didn't understand that God had not appointed him as gatekeeper for the Kingdom. It wasn't his job to see who got in and who was kept out. Simon didn't understand that his only responsibility was to be sure *he* got in, and he wasn't doing a good job there, either.

So, he did what many other self-righteous people have done over the years: Simon complained. He went to Jesus and whined about the woman who had crashed his party. I can imagine a mixture of indignant huffing and spineless whining:

"She doesn't deserve to be here; no one invited her. Her kind will ruin our reputation. If we let her in, the place will be flooded with people just like her. I don't like how she worships; it is not decent. And the way she dresses is inappropriate."

---

[2] Scripture is adamant not one of us can boast about being righteous apart from Christ. Romans 3:23 places us all in the same camp.

When Jesus Gets Fed Up With Complaining

Occasionally, Jesus gets fed up with complaining. Complaining limits our chance of receiving anything from Him. That was the case here after Simon made his litany of complaints. *"Jesus answered and said to him, 'Simon, I have something to say to you'"* (Luke 7:40).

Jesus then told the story about the creditor and let Simon know he had not even provided the common courtesy of the day when this woman had gone out of her way to express love for the Lord. He let Simon know his religion was worthless; it was getting him nowhere. And then, in amazing grace, Jesus turned to the woman and, without saying these words, said, "Woman, I have a message for you too: You've been saved; go in peace."

The faith she displayed in pressing through the crowd and offering worship when others were being critical put her in a position for Jesus to speak new life into her wretched existence. Basically, Jesus said, "You can start over." What a declaration from the King of kings! That phrase echoes today, calling to all who dare step out and come to Jesus.

Regardless of what "they" say about you, Jesus opens up a way for you to come into His presence and be drastically changed. Stop worrying about the noise of those around you. Ignore them, press close to Jesus, and He will meet you face to face.

SERMON OUTLINE

Introduction: Jesus was invited to a dinner party by one of the Pharisees. We know him as Simon. There are similarities and differences in the Gospels about the dinner engagements of Jesus, enough so to reveal this dinner probably stood alone from the others. What is common among them is the arrangement of the diners and onlookers.

1. A DINNER GATHERING
   a. Conversations
   b. VIP
   c. Courses
2. A DISRUPTIVE GUEST
   a. Hope
   b. Chutzpah
   c. Hallelujah
3. A DISGRUNTLED GOVERNOR
   a. Comparing Losers
   b. Confused Logic
   c. Complaining Limits

Conclusion: We all owe far more than we have the capacity to repay. Jesus has the same response to give us as He gave the party crasher. "Go in peace" can be heard from Him today by anyone willing to press into His amazing presence. Stop worrying about the gawkers hanging around the party. They are not interested in His transforming presence enough to break through. It is time to stop allowing them to dampen your desire for God's best.

STUDY QUESTIONS

1. Note the differences and similarities between the stories about Jesus and His dining schedule.
2. Who might qualify as a "party crasher" in today's church? What reactions would be displayed if they showed up at your church this Sunday? In light of today's need for security in church, how can we be open for honest seekers and still protect the congregation?
3. Chutzpah! How can you display this quality in God's kingdom? How is it needed to obtain God's favor in your life?
4. Can you see where the story of this woman brings hope to everyone? How does her story open up hope in your life?
5. What do you imagine when you see the term *effusive worship*? Have you ever displayed this type of passion toward Jesus? Why or why not? How might you display your passionate worship before Jesus?
6. Complaining limits your chances of receiving from Jesus. Are there areas of your life marked by complaining? What can you do to remedy this miracle-limiting practice?

10

A DAY OF CONFRONTATION

Have you ever had "one of those days"? You know, a day when it seemed everyone and everything was against you? You were tired when you woke up. You burned the toast and spilled the coffee. Getting ready for work, you spilled more coffee on the only clean shirt you had in the closet. The car would not start or there was a flat tire. The empty-tank warning light was on, and you were running late. You were chewed out for being late again and found out some of your co-workers have been carrying on a whispering campaign behind your back. Actually, that kind of day has the makings of a good country song. If you don't believe me, ask Willie Nelson. He made a hit out of such a day.[1]

Welcome to just such a day in the life of Jesus. We will piece together a day from His life—a day of confrontation. This day will show us some nasty attitudes from the religious leaders, coupled with a frightening judgment pronounced on them from Heaven. Our texts are Matthew 12:22-50; Mark 3:20-35; and Luke 8:1-3, 19-21; 11:14-36.

A study of the chronological life of Christ reveals these events, spaced out in different locales by the varying writers, all took place in a very short span of time.

In all likelihood, these events comprise one day in His life. And what a day it turned out to be! I think this was one of those hinge-pin days on which His life swung. The confrontations, along with the judgments pronounced, marked a turning point

[1] Willie Nelson's song "The Last Thing I Needed The First Thing This Morning" became a massive hit in 1982.

in His life as well as the attitude of the religious leaders. After this day of confrontation, things would never be the same.

A Comment About Money

> Now it came to pass, afterward, that He went through every city and village, preaching and bringing the glad tidings of the kingdom of God. And the twelve were with Him, and certain women who had been healed of evil spirits and infirmities — Mary called Magdalene, out of whom had come seven demons, and Joanna the wife of Chuza, Herod's steward, and Susanna, and many others who provided for Him from their substance (Luke 8:1-3).

The "afterward" in verse 1 reflects back to the preceding events: particularly a dinner at Simon's house and the anointing by a sinful woman. Luke elevated the common people, especially women, in his writings. He, more than any other Gospel writer, informs us how Jesus' ministry was funded. People gave to the traveling ministry of Jesus to keep it going. I don't doubt some of the twelve still had income from family fishing businesses[2], but the majority of support came from people whose lives were touched by His power and word.

That is, by the way, how God intends for His work to be financed. He intends for those blessed by the ministry of the local church to support the work. The idea that we draw our strength from one place but support another is not Biblical. We need to support the house where we are fed.

---

2 Mark 1:20 informs us Zebedee, the father of James and John, had a fishing business that employed servants to assist them.

A Frenzied Day

Now, our narrative begins to jump around. I am indebted to many sources for the outline of the chronology of His life. One great source, *The Chronological Life Of Christ* by Mark E. Moore, makes tracing the life of Christ much easier. We'll view Scripture passages as he blends narratives together.

> Then the multitude came together again, so that they could not so much as eat bread. But when His own people heard about this, they went out to lay hold of Him, for they said, "He is out of His mind" (Mark 3:20-21).

> Then one was brought to Him who was demon-possessed, blind and mute; and He healed him, so that the blind and mute man both spoke and saw. And all the multitudes were amazed and said, "Could this be the Son of David?" (Matthew 12:22-23).

The acts of ministry had reached a frenzied phase. It was so huge and overwhelming that Jesus and His disciples scarcely had time to eat or sleep. Jesus' half-brothers, who did not yet believe in Him, decided they had taken all the abuse they could stand. They took it upon themselves to stop all this fuss. They intended to take Jesus home by force if necessary.

I can imagine His brothers on the way to the house, fighting through the swelling crowds, talking smack among themselves. "I am going to talk some sense into Him," says one brother.

The second brother agrees, saying, "I am tired of Mother hearing all these stories and worrying about Him. It's about time He thought of someone besides Himself!"

"You got that right," says the third brother. "All this stuff has gone to His head! It's time He returned to His roots and started building furniture again."

Seeing the huge crowd following Jesus, they devise a plan. “Get ready for a fistfight,” says the fourth brother. “This bunch isn’t going to just let Him go.”

“What if He refuses to come with us?” asks the first brother.

“We will manhandle him until He comes to His senses,” says number two.

Amazing, isn’t it? The brothers would fight through an unruly crowd who wanted to get to Jesus as much, if not more, than any of them. Once inside, there was a secondary picket line called the disciples, who could be a rowdy group themselves. The brothers were going to take down Someone who had turned water to wine, handled evil spirits by a simple word, touched lepers and made them clean, and raised the dead? They were going to impose their will on *Him*? It would be like a six-ounce mouse striding up to a six-hundred-pound lion and taking him on. No contest!

Here’s what I can deduce from their actions and attitudes. First, they didn’t buy into who He was. They didn’t believe in Him. Second, what they had seen and heard, they readily dismissed.

What does that have to do with you and me? When we encounter a move of God in our lives, some will oppose what the Lord wants to accomplish. And those most vehemently against what the Lord wants to accomplish in our lives will often be those closest to us. Many times, the greatest opposition to you following the Lord in radical discipleship will be those from your own family.

Regrettably, I have witnessed this happen repeatedly through the years. I’ve watched on as someone came to the Lord, was on fire for God, and instead of their companion getting excited about it, confrontation developed.

It is a common scene acted out in many churches. Someone in a family, usually the wife, begins to walk with the Lord. As the fire of the Lord begins to burn, the spouse feels left out and grows sullen. He finally comes to church, perhaps after constant begging. His spiritually dead or lukewarm state makes him feel like a piece of bacon in a frying pan. He feels hot, bothered, and on display. In short, the move of God that happens when people come together to worship makes him uncomfortable.

The spouse (sometimes it's the wife), who is lost or so lukewarm that she can't stand being around any fire, says to her husband, "I don't like all that emotional, spiritual stuff." Then, the clincher comes in one of two ways: "I will go with you if you go to _____ church," or "If you go back there, I will _____ (insert a threat)."

Either way, pressure is used to draw the spouse away from the fire of God. Sometimes, the lost companion carries out their threat. They create great difficulty, even to the point of desertion, if the on-fire companion doesn't back down.

Here's where becoming a disciple of Christ can get tough. You must make up your mind. No one can do it for you. You must decide what's most important in your life. It may boil down to choosing your walk with God or giving in to someone who doesn't love the Lord. Such a decision has been forced on people for a long, long time.

Some of us must make some hard choices. We are going to be faced with the pressure of peers and family against the pressure of knowing God and having our children know the Lord. Heaven and hell are at stake in our decisions. Either we follow Christ, accepting Him and His direction, or we choose our own path, which is fraught with danger.

I am not implying you must go to my church to go to Heaven. I cannot guarantee that your children will be on fire and go to Heaven if they come to my church. But I can guarantee you this: Take them out of church because of family pressure, drag them to some dead church that has a form of godliness but denies the power of the Holy Spirit, and the enemy will consume them like a hungry child eats cookies for a snack.

My paternal grandfather, while dying, called his eight children around his bed. He had them swear allegiance to his church. I know the church. It's a dead relic of what it used to be, a place totally resistant to any move of God. But he had them swear to him upon his deathbed that they would never leave that church.

Through his eight children, I have fifteen first cousins. Five of those eight stayed in that church, or churches like that one, for the rest of their lives or else came into the fire of God late in life. From those five children, thirteen of my cousins were born. As best as I can tell, only one of them attends church. Tracing the lineage to second cousins, only one or two out of twenty are walking with God. An old man's dying wish was granted, but what a price will be paid in eternity!

Again, keeping your family in the fire of God is not a guarantee they will grow up and become devoted disciples. There are those raised in the fire who no longer walk with the Lord. But just the averages point to a sobering fact. Take your family away from a move of God, and you all but ensure their departure from the faith!

As important as your family and your friends are, there is One who lays a greater claim to our lives. We must make the choice to be related to Jesus. When He was told, *"Your mother and Your brothers are standing outside, desiring to see You"* (Luke

8:20), Jesus answered them, *"My mother and My brothers are these who hear the word of God and do it"* (v. 21).

I plan to be Jesus' "brother" by hearing from Him and doing what He says. What more could I want?

Family Conflict

While Jesus spoke about who was and was not part of His family, some in the crowd brought a pitifully bound man to Him. This poor guy was possessed by a spirit that made him blind and unable to speak. As soon as he got into the presence of Jesus, the Lord set him free. Suddenly, this man could both see and speak. The event was overwhelming to the watching crowd. They were *"amazed"* (Matthew 12:23). This wasn't something that just made them say "wow" and go on. This shook them so much that they lost control of their senses. Couching their reaction in Pentecostal language, we would say, "They had church!"

Suddenly, it clicked. "Could this really be Him? Do you think He might really be Messiah? Is all this we have heard about Him true?" Multitudes of people gathered around Him. Hundreds, if not thousands, crammed the streets where He walked. His power was undeniable. His ability was unlimited. Was it possible He was the long-awaited prophet of God?

In our attempts to rationalize the irrational, we often forget a foundational fact of the Gospels. The work of God does not stand on logic, education, money, prestige, or programs. Rather, it rises or falls on the demonstration of God's power in changed lives. This man's changed life drove them to the question of whether or not Jesus was who He claimed to be. Similarly, it will not be our great logic, our polished sermons, or our gifted choirs that bring people to Christ. It has been, and will forever be, changed lives that truthfully testify of Him.

People will flock to what makes them well. If you don't believe me, visit any doctor's office during flu season. The crowds swell because sickness drives us to what makes us feel better. Years ago, while still in high school, I learned a great lesson. It was a cold winter morning. I was running an early morning errand before school. Passing by the office of Dr. Bruce Russell (the only doctor in the area at that time), I saw a line of nearly fifty people standing against a wall, waiting for his office to open. Out in the frigid air for two or three hours, they steeled themselves against the elements in hopes relief would soon come their way.

As I saw them, the Holy Spirit whispered to my heart that if we could help people understand Jesus' wonderful healing power and the great change He can make in their lives, they would line up to get to Him. We should let people know a Healer is indeed in the house. They can come and receive more than a lecture about God; they can meet with God. We don't have to settle for hearing about what God once did; we can meet with Him today and He will do in our lives what needs to be done.

All around His church are testimonies of how Christ can still change lives. He can reach into the blindness of our lives and cause us to see. He can open the dumbness of our mouths and fill them with glorious praise. May He raise churches with such a glorious testimony to His awesome power!

Make no mistake, however—opposition will arise to such a display of His glory in our midst. Not only will there be people within who will seek to battle a move of God, but lurking around the sidelines will be those who directly oppose anything God wants to do. In other words, enter the Pharisees.

What happened next on this day of confrontation is both alarming and enlightening. Basically, the Pharisees hardened themselves in rejection of Jesus, who laid the wood to the fire of their judgment. They could not stand Jesus and sought to destroy Him at every turn. They didn't understand they were teetering on the edge of a chasm no one could cross. They were about to fall off a ledge and would not be rescued.

Their first mistake was denouncing Jesus worked by the Spirit. There was no way they could deny the work. A blind man could not see nor speak, but now he could do both. There was no way around such evidence. In much the same way today, there are multitudes of examples that Jesus changes lives. It's not hard to find drug addicts who have been set free, prostitutes who have been cleansed, and demon-possessed people who have been liberated. Churches are filled with sinful, spiteful, shameful sinners who were miraculously saved and made different. Don't buy into the story that Jesus doesn't do miracles today; He does.

Since the Pharisees couldn't deny the work, they had to denigrate it.

> Now when the Pharisees heard it they said, "This fellow does not cast out demons except by Beelzebub, the ruler of the demons." But Jesus knew their thoughts, and said to them: "Every kingdom divided against itself is brought to desolation, and every city or house divided against itself will not stand. If Satan casts out Satan, he is divided against himself. How then will his kingdom stand? And if I cast out demons by Beelzebub, by whom do your sons cast them out? Therefore they shall be your judges. But if I cast out demons by the Spirit of God, surely the kingdom of God has come upon you. Or how can one enter a strong man's house and plunder his goods, unless he first

> binds the strong man? And then he will plunder his house. He who is not with Me is against Me, and he who does not gather with Me scatters abroad" (Matthew 12:24-30).

The name *Beelzebub* carries numerous shades of meaning. "The Lord of the Flies" is one of the more prevalent meanings. Some say this day of confrontation was marked by an unusually large gathering of flies, and the Pharisees tried to tie Jesus to those pesky insects. The simple truth was they identified the work of Jesus with Satan. They said Jesus was doing Satan's work.

Jesus turned their logic around on them. He basically responded: "You say I do this by the power of Satan. That would be stupid. Would Satan be destroying his own empire? Finally, these other guys who are doing the same are your relatives. Are they full of Satan as well?"

Jesus then gave a powerful picture of spiritual warfare. He talked about a strong man. We know him as Satan. Jesus described him as mighty and quite capable. His house of great wealth is guarded, protected, and able to withstand an assault. If you wanted to take away that man's goods, you had to first deal with the man. You had to tie him up and render him powerless before you could take away his possessions.

Jesus gave us a strategy for victory. The only way to get anything back from Satan is to go in, bind him, and then take away what he has accumulated. If we think things will just come our way because we are believers, we need to rethink our position. The devil will not give us anything except a hard time.

You and I have to muster the courage to use the weapons made available to us to invade and conquer his domain and claim what belongs to Christ. That sounds ominous, and it can be. To take on such a project alone is foolish and dangerous. But, to those who align themselves with Jesus, there's nothing to fear. Regardless of the image of Satan as the big, bad wolf of our day, he has already been handled.[3] Here's some news that should elicit a worshipful response from all who love the Lord. Jesus has already bound Satan (Colossians 2:15), destroyed his works (1 John 3:8), and freed Satan's captives (Hebrews 2:14-15). Jesus has already judged Satan, declaring him cast out and defeated (John 12:31).

It is time we, the children of God, wake up and realize our foe has already been defeated. All he has against us—those covered with the blood of the Lamb—is deception. He cannot conquer us. He will try to convince us there is no way out, so we will give up. He will attempt to create such despair in us that we stop praying. He will attempt to weary us so we will cease to fight.

That's all he can do if we are married to Jesus. Jesus defeated Satan, and he knows it. He just wants us to forget that fact so we will act like he has the upper hand. Here's some uplifting news from 1 John 4:4: Greater is the One within us than the one who fights against us. We should stand our ground and see the salvation of the Lord.

A Frightening Situation

If you remember the old television series *Lost in Space*, you probably recall the silly-looking robot who was good for one thing. He knew when to say, "Danger, Will Robinson! Danger!" Some of the men standing in the presence of Jesus that day of confrontation are languishing in hell today, probably wishing someone had shouted "danger" at them. What happened next

---

[3] Matthew 12:28 informs us Jesus cast out demons by the Spirit of God. That's the same Spirit who indwells the believer.

goes down as one of the most controversial things Jesus ever did or said.

> "Therefore I say to you, every sin and blasphemy will be forgiven men, but the blasphemy against the Spirit will not be forgiven men. Anyone who speaks a word against the Son of Man, it will be forgiven him; but whoever speaks against the Holy Spirit, it will not be forgiven him, either in this age or in the age to come" Matthew 12:31-32).[4]

If there is a passage that causes more consternation than this one, I am unaware of its existence. This needs to be looked at closely for two reasons. First, it lets some people know they are not guilty and can relax. Second, we can fully understand what it means and not commit this horrible sin.

Jesus didn't speak this in a vacuum. He didn't wake up one morning and utter some obscure truth, something to make us all quiver. Instead, He tied this hard fact to what the Pharisees had said. The word *"therefore"* in Matthew 12:31 points us directly back to what just happened.

Jesus made it clear He was doing the works of God. He was bringing the kingdom of God to the earth. Since He was binding the strong man and plundering his domain, everyone (especially the Pharisees) had to make a choice: either side with Him or fight against what He was doing in the Spirit. Jesus was identifying their war against Him as blaspheming the Holy Spirit. While Jesus was warring in tandem with the Holy Spirit, they equated His works with demonic activity. Their attitude led to this reaction: "We don't accept you as Messiah. Since you are not the Messiah from God, you must

---

[4] Mark 3:30 adds that they said Jesus had an evil spirit.

be from Satan." On the heels of their rejection, Jesus gave an ominous warning.

Numerous times over the years, people from various walks of life have come to me in fear that they had committed this horrible sin. Beaten down and carrying guilt, they surmised they were past receiving forgiveness because of something they had done or said, usually in ignorance. Therefore, we need to understand what Jesus meant.

Jesus did not say the Pharisees had committed this sin, only that the commission of this sin leads to destruction. Knowing from the Scriptures that Jesus didn't mince words, had they actually committed this sin, wouldn't He have told them on the spot? I believe He would have nailed them, put them in their place, and made an example of them. If the things they said had made them ineligible for Heaven, Jesus would have made that clear.

I believe Jesus was warning them and us about the danger of the continued rejection of His work and lordship. Blasphemy against the Holy Spirit is a cynical unbelief that chooses to reject Him despite the evidence pointing to His reality. Here's the scary part: We do not have to say one word for this sin to harden us to the point of no return. It is possible to "blaspheme the Holy Spirit" without ever uttering one word.

The ultimate meaning of *blasphemy* is "to speak with irreverence against God." But a person's words only reveal his heart (see Luke 6:45). If someone speaks out against the Holy Spirit's work by calling it devilish, he is in danger. This danger does not begin when his vocal cords vibrate and sounds emit from his mouth, speaking against God. The intent and sentiment existed in his heart before words evidenced his belief.

I remember years ago sitting in my car listening to a radio preacher from another city having a field day denouncing Pentecostals and Charismatics. It wasn't just that he disagreed with me that was bothersome; he called me "devil-possessed." He stated that I and the millions of others of like faith were given over to Satan and demons because we sought the fullness of the Holy Spirit. He was caustic in his accusations, and it bothered me to the point that I prayed about it. Strangely enough, I called on the same Jesus he preached about.

What came into my spirit has sustained me through many other such attacks. It was as if the Lord whispered, "How can something from the enemy cause you to want to pray more, dig more into the Word, love Me more, long for My coming more, and want to win others to the cross more?" That settled the issue for me. And, while I am not that preacher's judge, I don't want to associate anything Jesus is doing through the power of the Holy Spirit with Satan. By the same token, I don't plan to sit quietly and let my heart grow so hard toward Jesus that it equates to saying something really stupid. I don't want to reach a point of being "unforgivable." Do you?

How does that come about? How does someone reach the point of becoming unforgivable in the eyes of God?

Several things need to be understood. First, the Holy Spirit is the last line of calling and conviction from God. It is His job to lead people to faith in Christ.[5] It is His job to convince someone of their need for salvation. While He often uses people to impart information and give invitations, the Holy Ghost is assigned the task of convincing unbelievers of the truth and convicting them of sin. Reject Him at this point, and there is no other way to be

[5] John 16:7-13 outlines the ministry of the Holy Spirit. First in line is His job of conviction, or convincing, that we need Christ.

saved. Reject His advances and there is no hope of salvation, for there is no other way a man can come to Christ.

Second, without repentance, there can be no forgiveness of sin. "Blasphemy against the Holy Spirit" is a rebellious and consistent rejection of the need to repent.

Third, if a person persists in such a hardened state of rebellion against God, he can become unreachable. He views evil as good and good as evil. His heart is so darkened and hard that the most unrelenting calls of the Holy Ghost go unrecognized.[6] Such a person is hopeless and will not turn to Christ and is thus unforgivable.

My fear is not that someone says something stupid and now desires forgiveness, but God stubbornly says "no." I fear people in the church today will be so stubborn and resistant to the Spirit that despite all the teaching and preaching, tremendous singing and worship, and fellowship and camaraderie, they will harden themselves to the wooing of the Holy Spirit and go into eternity without ever having repented.

As you read these words, are you faced with the haunting memory of something you said or did in the past and now wonder, *Did I commit that sin?* If so, answer these questions: Do you want to be saved? Do you have a desire to go to Heaven? Is it in your heart to repent and be forgiven? If so, guess who placed that hunger there? *Satan?* He won't do anything to shove you an inch closer to God. *Yourself?* We are "dead" in sin, unable to please God at all. No, there's nothing good in ourselves to draw us to God. *The Holy Spirit?* I think you are getting warmer.

If you aren't pushing yourself toward God, and Satan isn't pushing you toward Him, that leaves one entity. Enter the Holy Ghost. Since it's His job to draw you closer to the Father, to

---

6 Paul would render him given over to a "depraved mind" (Romans 1:28).

bring you salvation, and to present you faultless before the Almighty, He must be at work in your life if you want to go to Heaven. The devil is a liar and will use any trick to keep you away from Christ. Don't let him use this one on you. The reason you want to be saved is because you *can* be. Make no mistake, Satan knows it.

That's good news. The Holy Spirit is drawing you precisely because you are salvageable. Now, it's up to you. You can resist, which will ultimately result in what Jesus called "blasphemy against the Holy Ghost," or you can yield to the One who will defeat the enemy's power in your life. Millions of people all over the earth are happy they've chosen the latter. Join us. You won't regret a moment of service you give to the Master.

The religious leaders' second mistake was demanding a sign from Jesus. A demon had been cast out of a man a few moments before their confrontation, and the man stood there as a witness to Jesus' power. Previously in their region, Jesus had turned water to wine, read minds, healed all kinds of sicknesses, and cast out numerous demons. They had seen the cleansed lepers and chatted with those healed of paralysis and blindness. They heard how Jesus raised the son of the widow of Nain from the dead. Still, they did not believe Him. They demanded more. Regardless of the miracles, they were not convinced. Jesus turned the spotlight of discernment on them and launched into a tirade that left them reeling.

> Then some of the scribes and Pharisees answered, saying, "Teacher, we want to see a sign from You." But He answered and said to them, "An evil and adulterous generation seeks after a sign, and no sign will be given to it except the sign of the prophet Jonah. For as Jonah was three days and

> three nights in the belly of the great fish, so will the Son of Man be three days and three nights in the heart of the earth. The men of Nineveh will rise up in the judgment with this generation and condemn it, because they repented at the preaching of Jonah; and indeed a greater than Jonah is here. The queen of the South will rise up in the judgment with this generation and condemn it, for she came from the ends of the earth to hear the wisdom of Solomon; and indeed a greater than Solomon is here" (Matthew 12:38-42).

In response to their aggravating question, Jesus shot an answer back at them that seems a bit puzzling. They wanted another healing, some spectacular event. Jesus pointed to His future and told them to watch for an empty tomb. They wanted some great sign. He urged them to look for His resurrection. Why would Jesus do this?

For some, no matter what God does, it's never enough. That's how the Pharisees were. Jesus could have healed every sick person in Israel and turned the Red Sea into red wine, and it still wouldn't have been enough. Sure, they would have enjoyed the show, but they wouldn't accept His lordship.

In our age, we face the same situation. Tens of thousands will throng to "healing crusades" in hopes of getting or seeing a miracle, but they refuse to fall under discipleship in a local church. Millions rush to sanctuaries to hear the latest "feel good" messenger or take in the sharpest Chrisian entertainer but decline to make Jesus the Lord of their lives. They love the signs but reject the submission.

Miracles will not convince some people. That's what this day of confrontation revealed. In the story of the rich man and

Lazarus, the rich man in hell cried out for intercession for his brothers. That was probably the first time in his existence that he prayed for them, and it was too late. According to Jesus, it's possible to witness the most profound miracles and still miss God by a mile (see Luke 16:31).

I can't think of any miracle greater than someone who has been dead for decades suddenly popping up and preaching. I was just a boy when John F. Kennedy was assassinated. If he were raised from the dead and showed up in a service to tell about the afterlife and how the Lord wants to save us, I would let him have the floor and listen with rapt attention. Yet Jesus said some people would not be convinced by such a miracle. It's not because the miracle wasn't real, or because the Lord didn't want them saved, or because the Holy Spirit wasn't working to draw them in. It's because they had resisted to the point that they were unforgivable. Oh, may we learn to have tender hearts and passionate desires to know and serve the Lord!

Jesus did point them to a great sign that they rejected then and many cast aside today. It's the empty tomb. Easter is the capstone of everything with Christ's name on it. Everything in the Bible hinges on what happened in the pre-dawn darkness that first Sunday morning. None of us will ever see a greater miracle than that one. The fact that God raised Him from the dead after He had carried all our sins to the cross is the singular miracle of history.

All the other miracles of history have faded. Those who were healed of some disease got sick again and died. Those who had financial needs met were faced with some other need later on in life. Those who experienced great deliverance faced another giant on another day. Those who were set free from Satan's grip had to fight another battle. But the tomb remains vacant!

Nothing will ever change that. Nothing will ever outdistance that greatest of all signs. He was raised for us.

Avoid This Mistake

Don't make the same mistake many make. Don't believe the lie that you can get saved and then just go your way, doing whatever you want, and all will be fine. There's a grave danger out there, especially for those who have experienced the Lord's deliverance. Jesus said:

> "When an unclean spirit goes out of a man, he goes through dry places, seeking rest, and finds none. Then he says, 'I will return to my house from which I came.' And when he comes, he finds it empty, swept, and put in order. Then he goes and takes with him seven other spirits more wicked than himself, and they enter and dwell there; and the last state of that man is worse than the first. So shall it also be with this wicked generation" (Matthew 12:43-45).

Something miraculous has happened—a demon has been dislodged. A greater power than the devil has come by and set someone free. No doubt, it was a time of great rejoicing. Jesus then gave us a glimpse into the actions of this man, which mirrors the actions of so many touched by His hand. It's all wrapped up in one word: *empty.* What happened? Someone was willing to be delivered but content to exist without fellowship. He gladly welcomed deliverance but shunned discipleship. He was willing to live alone. He concluded that all he would ever need is the recollection of a wonderful act of God on his behalf.

But an unscheduled visit loomed on the horizon. The demonic force that had been driven out was planning a return. Only this time, things were going to be worse. Finding the house he once occupied clean but empty, the demonic spirit called for a party of his cohorts, and the empty place was filled. In the end, things were worse than ever.

What a shockingly accurate portrayal of the church world today. Millions of God's children seem blissfully ignorant of the danger of being empty and willing to live alone. The modern church wants to handle everything with the power of self. We feverishly work on every task with energy derived from our own ingenuity. We exclude worship, the Word, and the warmth of companionship at the Father's table every week. Unwittingly, we leave ourselves open for a greater attack than anything we've ever experienced.

A glaring example of this comes from Mobile, Alabama. A once-powerful pastor—a godly, Spirit-filled man—lay dying of cancer. As his friends gathered in his house, praying, singing, and worshiping around his bed, they did not expect him to see another sunrise. Emaciated and weakened, he was dying. Only, he didn't die. He did make it through the night. Awakening the next morning, he sat up and asked for some food. He got out of bed with help, and he started down a miraculous road of recovery that left him totally healed.

One would think this powerful recovery would result in a lifetime devoted to telling the story of the God who heals. Regrettably, this was not the case. Sometime later, the man who was near death but experienced great healing decided he no longer wanted to serve the Lord who raised him. He simply walked away, or at least that was how it appeared. The truth is that he was visited, and the evil ones found his house empty. Healed but empty. He fell, and "great was [his] fall" (Matthew 7:27).

From this day of confrontation in the life of Jesus, coupled with our own life experiences, we should come away with a new awareness of our need for sensitivity to the Spirit of God. We can ill afford to offend Him, to shut down His work in our lives, lest we cross an unseen line and reach a point of no return. That's scary, I know. But a greater risk, in my judgment, is the sobering fact that many of us are attempting to pull off what can't be done. Jesus has touched us. Set us free. Cleansed us. However, instead of filling our lives with Him and constantly immersing our souls in His strengthening power, we attempt to keep our options open and our houses cleaned for the next visitor who might come along.

Your house and mine, too, will be filled with someone. Success or failure and Heaven or hell depend on whom we allow to fill our lives. What you fill your house with, be it carnal or spiritual, holy or hellish, divine or demonic, will determine the rise and fall of your entire being. May He find us constantly crying out for more of Him.

SERMON OUTLINE

Introduction: Have you ever had "one of those days"? Not even the Son of Man was immune from hectic, demanding days. Before this day ended, Jesus would encounter nasty attitudes and accusations from the legalists, and He would make a frightening pronouncement of judgment on them. After this day, things would never be the same. His march toward the cross was becoming clearer with each passing incident.

1. A FRENZIED DAY
   a. Fast and Furious
   b. Friends and Foes
   c. Family and Followers
2. A FAMILY CONFLICT
   a. Disbelief of the Word
   b. Dismissing the Evidence
   c. Divisions Impacting Eternity
3. A FRIGHTENING CONSIDERATION
   a. Defeating the Enemy
   b. Danger of Eternal Judgment
   c. Desiring to Draw Near

Conclusion: Jesus' amazing day of conflict teaches we must remain sensitive to God's Word and the moving of His Spirit in our lives. We cannot afford to shut Him out, lest we find ourselves crossing some unseen line and moving past a point of no return. Our enemy is waiting for us to leave our house "empty" so he might destroy us. Such action is impossible for those filling their houses with the treasures of God's Word and His Spirit!

STUDY QUESTIONS

1. Have you ever been guilty of allowing a busy day or season to distract you from your spiritual pursuits? What caused you to awaken to the drift in your life? What actions did you take to remedy the situation?
2. How do you personally fund the work of the Gospel? What does your giving, or lack thereof, say about your gratitude?
3. What might have been key factors in the disbelief of Jesus' half-brothers? Do any of these same factors work against your faith?
4. Do you think anyone who has crossed the line of God's mercy would ever seek forgiveness? Why or why not?
5. How does the teaching of Jesus on spiritual warfare apply to our lives? Give an example of how we might engage in a spiritual battle.

KINGDOM STORIES

> And the disciples came and said to Him, "Why do You speak to them in parables?" He answered and said to them, "Because it has been given to you to know the mysteries of the kingdom of heaven, but to them it has not been given. For whoever has, to him more will be given, and he will have abundance; but whoever does not have, even what he has will be taken away from him. Therefore I speak to them in parables, because seeing they do not see, and hearing they do not hear, nor do they understand. And in them the prophecy of Isaiah is fulfilled, which says: 'Hearing you will hear and shall not understand, And seeing you will see and not perceive; for the hearts of this people have grown dull. Their ears are hard of hearing, and their eyes they have closed, lest they should see with their eyes and hear with their ears, lest they should understand with their hearts and turn, so that I should heal them.' But blessed are your eyes for they see, and your ears for they hear; for assuredly, I say to you that many prophets and righteous men desired to see what you see, and did not see it, and to hear what you hear, and did not hear it" (Matthew 13:10-17).

Jesus had quite a day. Starting with a massive blow-up with the religious elite, He then cured a man of a demonic possession that had rendered him mute and deaf. Moving further into the day, He preached a sermon using stories to challenge His hearers. He later moved on to calm a storm. To make the day complete, He marched ashore and performed a miracle that is my favorite story about Jesus. If you told me I only had one day to follow Jesus, this day would be my choice.

Coming off the accusations of the Pharisees and His stern warning about crossing a line with God, Jesus began another sermon by using stories the Bible calls "parables."[1] Parables are stories using symbols to illustrate a truth. As we will see, Jesus used seven short stories to communicate powerful truths about the kingdom of God.

All around Him were enactments of the stories He told. From the shelter of a boat, He could point to farmers sowing seed and fields growing with a mixture of grain and weeds. There were vacant areas in every direction where a buried treasure could be found, and they all ate bread in which leaven had been used. Meanwhile, the seashore was teeming with fishermen and their nets—men busily trying to draw a living from the waters. This mishmash of day-to-day events provided the Master Teacher with ample illustrations of grand spiritual truths. In our day of trying to impress and "out-inform" the next guy, we probably make the Kingdom too complicated. Jesus, the One who purchased the Kingdom and keeps it all going, was able to point to a guy's garden and dispense so much truth that millennia later, we are still excavating truth from His words.

Mysteries

I confess a similarity with the disciples at this point. Why did Jesus shift from straightforward teaching to wrapping up truth in stories that must be explained?

---

[1] A parable is a story used to convey a spiritual truth. For the differences between parables, myths, proverbs, and allegories, see R. C. Trench, *Notes on the Parables of Our Lord*.

Why change from His last great sermon, where He was so explicit and concise and ordered us to pray for people who mistreat us? Why switch to this new model of telling a story and demanding we dig in to obtain the truth? In essence, this is what the disciples asked Jesus in the setting that opens this chapter.

Jesus taught them the reason He began to speak in parables was to fulfill Isaiah 6:9-10: *"Go, and tell this people: 'Keep on hearing, but do not understand; Keep on seeing, but do not perceive.' Make the heart of this people dull, and their ears heavy, and shut their eyes; lest they see with their eyes, and hear with their ears, and understand with their heart, and return and be healed."*

According to Jesus, the reason He taught in parables was twofold. First (and this is the negative aspect), the Pharisees had become so dull and hardened that they would not receive the truth. They simply passed off all He said as the ramblings of a madman and dismissed Him out of hand. However, they would not be able to stand before God and claim they had been mistreated. No, they would hear the truth, but their dullness would prevent them from grasping the powerful message taught by Jesus.

Second (and this is very positive), the truth of the Kingdom has been given to us. The mysteries of the Kingdom are ours for the taking, but we are required to dig to obtain truth.

We must remain open to truth and have a willingness to change our lives as God leads us into a deeper walk with Him. We cannot afford to grow stagnant or reach the place where we think there is nothing else left for us to learn. That's one reason Jesus taught in parables—they open us up to new revelations. They assist us in a new consideration of God's kingdom. None of us should consider ourselves to have achieved that lofty and deadly perch of completion, so let's read the Apostle Peter's message:

> But also for this very reason, giving all diligence, add to your faith virtue, to virtue knowledge, to knowledge self-control, to self-control perseverance, to perseverance godliness, to godliness brotherly kindness, and to brotherly kindness love. For if these things are yours and abound, you will be neither barren nor unfruitful in the knowledge of our Lord Jesus Christ. For he who lacks these things is shortsighted, even to blindness, and has forgotten that he was cleansed from his old sins. Therefore, brethren, be even more diligent to make your call and election sure, for if you do these things you will never stumble; for so an entrance will be supplied to you abundantly into the everlasting kingdom of our Lord and Savior Jesus Christ (2 Peter 1:5-11).

Do you know the "reason" Peter references in verse 5? Looking back a couple of verses, the aged apostle said God has already given us everything we need to be full of the Spirit and obtain the promises made. The Lord has even provided us with all we need to escape the corruption that permeates the world. That being the case, we are called upon to get up and do something about all God has given us.

We need to stop living in the fantasy world that because we have experienced some "event" with God, we have no further need. We need to put to rest the idea that because we once were "converted" or "spoke in tongues" or even had a "sanctification" experience, we need no more growth. The idea that an event equals a status of no more spiritual diligence—no more dedication to delving into God's character and applying that learning—is alien to Scripture. It may be popular in some quarters, but it is not Biblical.

The Apostle Peter wrote to a group of saints forced to flee for their lives, who had laid it all on the line and who were filled with the Spirit: *Keep on adding to your spiritual life, so you don't stumble and fall!*

Keep adding, keep digging. We are doing protective work. If we don't, Peter says we are blind and ignorant. He warns trouble is coming our way. Conversely, if we are willing to dig, listen, learn, and change, then powerful stability will be imparted. We are not going to stumble, and we will have an entrance into Heaven so grand it will blow our socks off!

Before we look at the seven stories Jesus told, there is a word from Him that haunts me (Matthew 13:22). In a sweeping statement, Jesus said those who have knowledge of God will be given more, even to the point of abundance. Those who refuse to know Him (including the Pharisees standing there), even what they have will be taken away. What haunts me is the possibility that a minister like me, one who supposedly knows God, can reach the place where I am no longer open to truth. I fear I could become so dull and set in my stubborn ways that I can no longer hear His voice. I shudder to think my church and my denomination can become so entrenched and stale that the Lord must take His hand from us because we no longer listen to His voice. May He find us eager to dig and ready to excavate from His stories the truths that will lead us to greater victory!

Measuring Results

Rather than taking this sermon verse by verse and story by story, let's consider three great truths from the whole. We could spend chapters exploring each individual parable. Theological systems have been erected on interpretations of these stories.

Our task is not to get bogged down in dissecting each word. Instead, I want to lift three truths about this Kingdom from His words and see what they can mean to us.

Up front, the Kingdom is about something gained. The two stories Jesus told in Matthew 13:44-46 illustrate this. In one short story, a man finds a hidden treasure in a vacant field. Realizing the value of the treasure, he immediately goes home, sells all he owns, and then purchases the empty lot. The other story is similar. In his busy attempts to find great bargains, a merchant happens upon a single pearl unlike any he has ever seen. Realizing the value of that pearl, he goes home and sells everything so he might obtain that jewel. In both cases, the moral is the same: *Pay whatever price we have to pay, give up whatever we have to give up, and do whatever we have to do, so we can obtain the Kingdom of God.*

The price paid for this Kingdom makes it worthwhile. In the story of the pearl, Jesus pointed to the pain and agony needed to bring about the purchase. An irritant is introduced into the oyster's shell. Covering the painful irritant with layer after layer of resplendent material, the oyster eventually produces a beautiful pearl. The pain produces the pearl; the irritant brings about the glory.

What a powerful illustration! We know the price Jesus paid for this Kingdom. It was not the miracles that bought us. It was not the great teaching that set us free. No, we have been purchased with Jesus' blood, shed on our behalf. It spurted from a painful, irritating set of wounds. As such, it is worth far more than any earthly treasure we can obtain.[2] His sacrifice makes this Kingdom worth whatever price we must pay to get in.

---

[2] First Peter 1:18-19 clarifies our salvation came not from earthly treasures, but from heavenly sacrifice.

In our day of "easy believe-ism," too many of us shrink back at the slightest hint of hardship or opposition. It's as if we in North America have concocted a gospel for "softies." We forget it's the irritants that produce pearls. Don't allow the costs associated with gaining the Kingdom keep you from getting in and staying in. The result will be worth whatever price you must pay.

Consider the man who bought the field. Headed home, he devised his business plan. The field cost a lot of money. The owner wouldn't let it go cheaply because it was probably bought for investment purposes. Figuring up what he had in the bank, the man fell far short of his goal. In his intense desire to buy the priceless field, he thought about selling his sheep, cow, goat, and three chickens. Still not enough. He could add the nice blankets he bought last month for the kids and the new clothes he bought his wife and himself for Passover. Still short. On top of all that, he could sell the donkey. Still not enough. If it had to be, it had to be: He would sell his house and all the furniture. Finally. He would have enough to buy the field.

Here's where things get dicey. He can't go blabbing about what he was doing. If he did, someone with more money than him would step up and buy the field. So, he had to endure the criticism of his wife, his kids, his neighbors, his in-laws, and his parents. In short, he had to be willing to pay the price of discomfort and misunderstanding to obtain what was priceless. People probably ridiculed him. We tend to do that when someone dares to operate outside our expected norms.

In 1867, the U.S. Secretary of State, William H. Seward, signed a treaty with Russia to purchase the huge territory of Alaska. He was besieged with catcalls and opposition. Labeled "Seward's Folly" and "Seward's Icebox," people were so adamant he was making a mistake that when the vote for the treaty was presented to the U.S. Senate, it passed by only one vote. The senators who railed against the two-cents-per-acre purchase have long since hidden themselves in the dustbins of history. Like the man in the story told by Jesus, Seward pushed through the negativity and made one of the greatest land purchases in history.

In the end, the man of whom Jesus spoke went out to his costly field with his shovel and family in tow and dug up a treasure that made them all fabulously rich. Guess who was laughing last? He had paid a great price, but he obtained a greater reward than any around him.

Is Christ's kingdom worth it? Is putting up with the abuse, the mockery, the misunderstanding, the mistreatment, and the sacrifice worth the cost? If you ask the man with the treasure, it was. If you ask the man with the pearl, it was. If you could ask saints of God from the past, regardless of how much suffering they endured, I'm sure their unanimous statement would be a bold "yes." In all your gaining, doing, and accomplishing, be sure you attain the greatest of all possessions: Christ in you, the hope of glory.

Obtaining the Kingdom (or perhaps better said, the Kingdom obtaining *you*) is not the end of God's purpose. Christ teaches that the Kingdom is about growing. This is where the bulk of this sermon rests. The kingdom of God is a growing, living thing. Applied globally, Jesus meant for His kingdom to expand until it reached all the earth.

The story of the mustard seed displays this wonderful truth.[3] Small in the beginning, much like the ministry of Jesus, the plant grows until many birds can come and find rest. The shade extends and provides comfort. In other words, the Kingdom,

---

[3] Matthew 13:31-32; Mark 4:30-32; Luke 13:18-19.

though small in inception, is intended to become something that extends far beyond its beginnings.

As an individual, the Kingdom is not something we take in and isolate. Nowhere is there a place for "compartmentalized Christianity" the world is willing to tolerate. Instead, this faith is like leaven going into bread.[4] *Leaven* is another word for *yeast*. Jesus likens the Kingdom in our lives to yeast in bread.

Ask any baker what yeast does. Yeast makes dough rise. Yeast makes dough mature. The yeast spreads until it affects the whole loaf. There's no half-yeast roll. Go to any restaurant that offers yeast rolls (which are devilishly delicious); you won't find any half-yeast rolls.

We need to dispense with this idea that we can divide our lives into "Kingdom" and "non-Kingdom" areas. That's what society will tolerate and accept, especially if you are a politician, but according to Jesus, such a Kingdom does not exist. It is impossible to be a Kingdom person on Sunday and a worldly person the rest of the week. Either the yeast of the Kingdom will affect your entire life, or it will die.

Did you know there are two ways to kill yeast? First, you could "starve" it by giving it nothing to grow through. Second, you could heat it until it dies alone. What a portrait of the spiritual life! How many fatalities have come about because we isolated the yeast of the Kingdom into a small part of our lives, thinking we could become divided servants? How many crashes have occurred in the spiritual world because we left the yeast of the Kingdom alone and allowed the pressure of life to burn it up?

Understand the teaching of Jesus. We are either growing up or going down. We are either becoming more and more concentrated with the Kingdom, or we are killing the influence

---

[4] Matthew 13:33; Luke 13:20-21.

of God in our lives. We are either becoming more and more influenced by Him, or we are killing the leaven of the Kingdom by isolation. Read any secular book you wish and study all the articles available about our current culture. They will inform you that a small dash of religion is tolerable, even desirable. We want leaders who tip their hats to God. We want a president who acknowledges the "Creator" who made us. Our culture says that's where it should end. Our religion should be something hidden from sight, undetectable in our worldview, and obscured from our decision-making process.

As much as I want to be accepted and have everyone like me, as much as I don't want to be pilloried in the press or laughed at by the "elite" of our society, I must hearken back to Jesus' teaching that this Kingdom will not sit idly in a hidden corner of my life and await my flippant decisions to come and go. Either it will inform every decision I make, or it will die. It will be seen in the way I act toward everyday life, or it will suffocate. It will permeate everything about me, or it will diminish into nothing. Jesus calls for complete access to every area of my life. Nothing less will do.

His story about the different types of soil is perhaps the Bible's greatest explanation of the Kingdom and how it functions. It is also the longest of His stories.[5] In this story, Jesus lumped humanity into four categories. First, there is the hard soil that can't receive any seed. The Word can fall on it, but it does no good. It sits idle, and Satan steals it before anything can happen. This person comes to church because someone begged him until he gave in. What is preached doesn't matter. All he can do is sit uninvolved until it is over. Leaving, the Word falls off. Satan picks the Word out of his life like birds picking up

[5] Matthew 13:3-9; Mark 4:1-9; Luke 8:4-8.

seed on a hard path. It's not the Word's fault, and I'm thankful it's not the sower's fault. The fault lies at the feet of the man who has grown so hard toward God that nothing can grow in his life. All the preaching in the world will do him no good until he softens himself and becomes willing to receive.

Second, there is the shallow soil. It seems good at first, but after a short while, something goes wrong. The thin layer on the top produces a seemingly quick harvest, but the underlying rock prevents any real growth. While volumes are written about this man, I view him as the fellow who makes an emotional move without ever considering what it will cost him. Unlike the men who sold all to purchase a field and a pearl, this guy is easily swayed. As soon as the cost of following Jesus is presented, he's gone. This explains why some people rush to an altar and pray, even cry, but three weeks later—sometimes one week later—they are gone. It's as if nothing happened to them at all. Once the emotion of the moment passed and the Word called for them to lie down and die, it was over. As before, neither the message nor the messenger is to blame—only the individual unwilling to prioritize God in their life.

The third soil really disappoints. Jesus said some people would produce and look good, but only for a while. Lasting longer than the previous, emotionally oriented individual, this person hangs in when things get dry. He has enough of God to last a while. But, as it inevitably happens, some stuff in life comes along and starts competing for time. That's what thorns and weeds do in a garden. They compete for life-giving nutrients. Over time, they will choke the life out of the intended plant. Jesus warned about allowing the cares of life to prevent us from growing. We can't afford to allow our pursuit of money, our longing for a career, or life's disappointments to stop us from growing and cause us to die.

One thing you can count on about weeds and other invasive plants is they don't stop growing! Recently, while on a deer stand, I observed a parasitic climbing vine on a tall tree. Intertwining itself with the tree's branches, the vine had reached far to the top of this giant tree. Already, this parasite vine was several inches in diameter and larger than most ropes. Over time, the mighty tree will succumb to the constant growth of the choking weed. If we stop growing in the Lord, stop surrendering our lives, cease feasting on His Word, and shut down our prayer life, then like the mighty oak in that river bottom, one day our life will be drained out of us by the cares of this world. When that oak falls one day during a storm, out there alone, no one will notice its passing. We have too many precious things around us to allow our lives to be cut short. We must keep growing!

Finally, there is good soil, which produces over time. This is what we all want to become—productive. Over the long haul, we want to make a difference for the Lord and have Him make a difference in us. Ultimately, my goal is to hear Him say I was productive in His Kingdom. It's up to me to be sure I keep growing.

Mastering

If only gaining and growing were the end of His stories. Alas, Jesus does not stop short. He goes on to inform us of the ugly truth about opposition—an opposition we must master. A member of my church once related a saying attributable to a former co-worker. This guy was fond of saying, "Ain't but two things you can count on: a sharp knife and a dollar bill. One can cut, and one can spend. Got both in my pocket." I hate to add to his sage wisdom, but here's something else you can count on: When you want to grow, you will encounter opposition.

In His story about the intruder who comes into a planted field and sows weeds, Jesus outlined many strategies of the opposition (Matthew 13:24-30).

First, our opposition will be subtle. Notice when the attack came. Everything happened at night while everyone was asleep. The enemy didn't come clanging gongs, shooting off rockets, or sending advance notice. They were very subtle and tactful in their approach. Creeping silently through the underbrush, they came armed with life-sapping resources, intent on destroying the growth. How many have fallen prey to the subtle intentions of the enemy? Honestly, I can handle a roaring lion. I know what to do if I hear a lion roaring and look outside and see him in the yard. I will get my large-caliber gun and shoot the intruder. It's the "angel of light" routine that scares me. It's the imperceptible slide, the little giving in to the seemingly harmless suggestions that causes me to step back and take note. It's the rationale offered for missing church, the excuses I can find for neglecting God's Word, the many reasons why I cannot pray, the pretexts I can proffer as to why I don't have the same passion for God that give me pause.

Second, the opposition will become sweeping. At first, it's subtle, imperceptible. But what happens next is frightening. Such an approach becomes obvious only with the passing of time. I know too many who have fallen hard after taking a few steps on the slippery slope of compromise, and I am aware of my weaknesses and how the enemy will work on me. Be sure of this: The tiny step, the slight indiscretion, the small slip, is not the final outcome. It won't end there. Not until the enemy has you down and destroyed will he be satisfied.

Third, wheat and tares will grow together. In the same church, under the same conditions, right under your nose, both will grow. That's what Jesus taught in Matthew 13:30. That verse answers a boatload of questions for me. As a pastor and leader in the church, it has been my unfortunate opportunity to be forced to deal with some ungodly attitudes and unchristian actions over the years. People have been harsh, mean, judgmental, and downright sinful while serving in prominent church positions. Like some of you, I have wondered why God puts up with it. Then again, I wonder why God puts up with me, but that's a different sermon.

Have you ever heard someone question why a liar, cheat, thief, adulterer, swindler, or some other unsavory character gets to serve on a church board? Has anyone ever pointed out to you the people in the church who are not living right? To add insult to injury, perhaps they blamed you, God, and the church for creating the problem. If so, you need to memorize this verse and learn to point out a couple of things.

First, Jesus is more concerned with preserving His tender harvest than shutting down a hypocrite. He will allow some fraudulent old cuss room to move around before He will risk killing some new baby in the Lord. That being a Kingdom truth, we should pray hard for a harvest of new believers!

Second, it's not my job or yours to worry about uprooting and sorting out the different plants. You and I need to be sure we are growing and leave the weeding out up to God. The day is coming when harvest will occur. In that time, you will want to be on the side of the grain. Speaking of that day in another location, Jesus gave a vivid image of what will happen: "*And then He will send His angels, and gather together His elect from the four winds, from the farthest part of earth to the farthest part of heaven*" (Mark 13:27).

Scattered around the world is the growing grain of God. Yes, there are tares in the wheat. Among us are hypocrites who appear to be just like the grain on Sunday but live like a weed through the week. Don't worry about the weeds; be sure you are grain. His angels know the difference, and they will only collect the true blue. Be sincere enough to take care of your own life and let God handle the rest, and you will be a happier believer!

One last story from this sermon. Pointing to fishermen separating their catches, Jesus illustrated what the Kingdom of God looks like:

> "Again, the kingdom of heaven is like a dragnet that was cast into the sea and gathered some of every kind, which, when it was full, they drew to shore; and they sat down and gathered the good into vessels, but threw the bad away. So it will be at the end of the age. The angels will come forth, separate the wicked from among the just, and cast them into the furnace of fire. There will be wailing and gnashing of teeth" (Matthew 13:47-50).

When all is said and done, when time is fully completed, God will do some serious separating. Moving among the billions of people who have lived, God's angels will make two groups (not three or four groups, but only two). Two choices, two possible endings. All sorts of people are in church today, but all are destined for one of two places. Some are headed to Heaven, while others are headed to hell.

It's probably been a long time since, if ever, some of you heard a message about hell. That's a shame because so many people are blindly going to that horrible place. The real shame is that no one has to go there. The price Jesus paid for us is enough. The life He calls for us to live is enough.

The details of this horrible eternity are sobering. Listen to the words employed by Jesus to describe the monstrosity of the place we call hell: weeping, wailing, gnashing of teeth, utter darkness, eternal torment, and angry flames. Hopeless agony forever. That's how hell is described. On the other hand, Heaven is talked about in such glowing terms that Paul, who visited it one time, said it was illegal even to speak of such a grand place.

Where are you going? One of the two, according to Jesus, awaits every person. I challenge you to take the stories of His Kingdom to heart and call on the One who paid so great a price for your salvation. Whatever it costs you to make it in, you will be glad you made the payment.

SERMON OUTLINE

Introduction: What a day Jesus had! A long, weary day, complete with virtually every emotion possible. During His tiring day, He launched into a sermon laced with *parables,* which are stories illustrating Kingdom truth. Everywhere He and they looked, men and women were acting out the stories He shared.

1. MYSTERIES
   a. Prophetic Fulfillment
   b. Perceivable Truths
   c. Protective Work
2. MEASURING THE KINGDOM
   a. Gaining in the Kingdom
   b. Growing in the Kingdom
   c. Grounds of the Kingdom
3. MASTERING OPPOSITION
   a. Subtle
   b. Sweeping
   c. Simultaneous

Conclusion: The impact of the Kingdom stories is simple. Eternity awaits us, and ensuring our location within His Kingdom outweighs any lofty goal or pursuit we can name. Nothing matters more than being part of the gathering who hear "Well done" on that last day. We must do whatever is required to be in that number.

STUDY QUESTIONS

1. Do you have a favorite parable from Jesus? What makes it stand out from the rest? What underlying but perceptible truths do you think Jesus is teaching from these stories?
2. What is your favored means of digging into God's Word for deeper truth? Do you have a preferred study method? Perhaps you can share with others the way you study Scripture and learn from them about the methods they enjoy.
3. Is there anything in your life of such value you would forsake God's Kingdom to obtain/retain it? Does your lifestyle reveal the truth about that question?
4. How do you respond to the truth that you were purchased and placed in Christ's Kingdom by blood? What do we owe Jesus for His ultimate sacrifice? Do you understand the difference between "paying Him back" and "living in gratitude"?
5. Does the yeast of the Kingdom affect every area of your life?
6. Which description of soils best describes your walk with Jesus? How can you assist in the receptivity of the soil in your life?
7. What opposition to the Kingdom are you currently experiencing? How can you better defeat that opposition?

12

WHEN A LONG DAY ENDS WITH A STORM

> On the same day, when evening had come, He said to them, "Let us cross over to the other side." Now when they had left the multitude, they took Him along in the boat as He was. And other little boats were also with Him. And a great windstorm arose, and the waves beat into the boat, so that it was already filling. But He was in the stern, asleep on a pillow. And they awoke Him and said to Him," Teacher, do You not care that we are perishing?" Then He arose and rebuked the wind, and said to the sea, "Peace, be still!" And the wind ceased and there was a great calm. But He said to them, "Why are you so fearful? How is it that you have no faith?" And they feared exceedingly, and said to one another, "Who can this be, that even the wind and the sea obey Him!" (Mark 4:35-41).

It may seem as if we are jumping all over the place in an effort to follow the tracks of Jesus. I guess we are. While we are attempting to follow Him chronologically, the writers of the Gospels were not concerned with a daily diary. Instead, they were interested in presenting Jesus as the Savior promised by God. They took stories of His life and lumped them together to suit their particular audience. That's why this event, which was part of one ongoing day in the life of Christ, seems misplaced. The "same day" we encounter here ties in with the already powerful and exhausting day spent by Jesus.

On this seemingly endless day, Jesus had confronted the Pharisees. Anyone who has been forced to undergo such attacks will testify to the physically taxing nature of such an ordeal. On top of that, He had cast out a devil from a man. No doubt this took power from his battery as well. Following on the heels of those events, He preached a powerful sermon, couched in parables. Any pastor can testify to the grinding nature of standing before people and doing the best job possible to represent God's truth. All these events had a cumulative effect on Jesus and wore Him down. Jesus, though God, was also a man. Like us, He grew weary.

So, the next time you are tired in church, don't feel so bad. If Jesus grew weary, it is okay for your energy level to wane. However, don't fall asleep. Once when Paul was preaching, a young fellow named Eutychus fell asleep, tumbled out of a third-story window, and broke his neck (Acts 20:7-12). Miraculously, Paul raised him from the dead. (However, if you fall asleep during my preaching, my feelings would be so ruffled I probably wouldn't be able to raise you!)

Worn out from His grueling day, Jesus told His disciples to use the boat He had been teaching from and travel to the other side of the Sea of Galilee. The trip was only a few miles, and the fishermen with Him had fished every inch of that water. It was going to be a piece of cake. At least, that's how it started.

At some point in the journey, someone uttered one of those famous "Oh no!" statements. The disciples knew in a moment what was happening. From out of nowhere, a storm blew up. The phrase "great windstorm" means a "mega wind." We would say a tornado, or huge waterspout, blew in on them.

The Sea of Galilee is a small body of water about thirteen miles long and seven miles wide. It sits almost 700 feet below sea level and has mountain ranges all around. Everyone from the southern United States knows what happens when cold air from the north meets hot air from the south. We have lived through storms—sometimes big, bad, killer storms. In essence, that's precisely what happened on this night. At the end of a long, hard day, a storm blew up.

Stormy Facts

I am not a fan of mega storms. I don't mind a little rain, even some thunder and lightning . . . as long as I can stay inside! But when the storms start raging and threaten my security, that's another matter. I am like the young boy whose mother put him to bed late one night when the storms were blowing outside. Frightened, the little fellow begged his mother, "Mom, stay with me! Sleep with me tonight!"

Knowing she had to instill courage in her son, Mom said, "Honey, I have to sleep with your daddy tonight." As she turned to leave the room, her son replied, "The big sissy!" Regardless of whether we are brave, we should look at some facts about storms before seeing the Peace-speaker in action.

- *Storms come.* They just happen. We live in an imperfect world, surrounded by imperfect people. I even have storm-causing potential myself. Until we get to Heaven, we will have storms.
- *Storms come to all.* You can't live holy enough, get sanctified enough, or get close enough to God to avoid storms. Forget the idea that you can fast and pray enough to prevent storms from coming your way. They will come to everyone, including every child of God.
- *Storms come when you least expect or want them.* That's precisely where we find Jesus and the disciples. They had been at it all day long. Jesus

had expended vast amounts of energy, and He was bone-weary. But that didn't stop the storm from coming His way.

- *Storms can come repeatedly.* Life has a way of piling on. When you are bone-weary, the enemy will cause a storm to blow up in your life. It's easy to see what happens in the natural mirrored in the spiritual. The hurricanes that hit the southeastern United States in 2024 didn't care that Florida had already been hit. They struck with savage fury. Also, spots in the U.S. known as "tornado alley" have been hit again and again. I can personally attest to killer tornadoes crossing the exact same areas in and around Birmingham, Alabama—the biggest city near my home.

  It's not uncommon for someone to tell their story and describe storm after storm. Sickness is followed by job loss, followed by financial disaster. Then come marriage problems, followed by problems with children. A drinking problem might be followed by drug problems, followed by legal problems. You get the idea. Life piles on. I know it's not fair, but whoever said life was going to be fair?

- *Storms always come to an end.* Some last longer than others, but storms must feed on some energy, and they all eventually run out of steam. Perhaps you are in the midst of the storm of the century. I assure you that it will end. You and I must find the stamina to last and the strength to hold on. Sooner or later, that storm you suffer today will cease, and the birds will sing again.

I love the promise in Psalm 30:5: *"Weeping may endure for a night, but joy comes in the morning."* If I can hold on through the night, if you can make it a few more hours, and if we can find the courage to stand in the wind and rain a little longer, the storm will subside. Joy will then come rushing in like the streams of sunlight erasing the darkness of another night.

Searching for Help

Once the disciples set sail for the other side of the Sea of Galilee, Jesus sat down and soon was sound asleep. Can anyone besides me identify with that? Some wives know all too well what happens when their husband gets in a recliner late in the evening. Also, some husbands know what happens when their wife gets in the passenger seat for a road trip. The result is the same: sleep.

In one part of the boat, Jesus was snoring. In the other part, the disciples were rowing. Out of nowhere, a dangerous storm came roaring. It was so dangerous that the fishermen who had spent their lives on these waters grew terribly afraid of death (Mark 4:38). The ship they relied on was headed for the bottom, carrying them with it. Disaster was headed their way, and they were powerless to change anything. No doubt they had tried all the usual measures. They worked hard bailing out water. They strained, trying to keep the ship upright. They were professionals and did all the things they knew to do.

This time, things were different. Nothing was working. Try as they might, they had reached the end of their abilities. It was hopeless.

Have you ever looked at a situation and muttered, "Hopeless"? You gave something your best effort only to fail. You thought you had it all worked out, but now it's all to pieces. The counseling didn't work. The systems you had in place fell apart. That medicine you took didn't have the hoped-for effect. Many of us face such a storm today. Facing overwhelming issues with no end in sight, hopelessness invades our dreams. Dealing with situations spiraling out of control, panic seems to be the order of the day. Looking at things with no foreseeable good conclusion, fear creeps into our dreams. Gripped by strongholds from which we cannot extricate ourselves, we exhaust ourselves with futile battle. To make matters worse, while we are floundering about, giving it our best shot, stretching and straining with all our might like the disciples that evening, it seems Jesus is asleep.

I am a realist. I can't stand it when some preacher or writer paints a rosy portrait of a syrupy faith and gooey existence they supposedly have with Jesus. Perhaps you know the type. They always live on top of every circumstance. One could kidnap their children, hold their wife hostage, shoot their dog, burn down their church, send them a letter laced with anthrax, withhold food and water, and they would be on top of the world, singing praise songs and walking in joyous smiles. You know the type. They never have a bad hair day. They never get a speeding ticket. Their kids never give them one moment's trouble. They say it's all because of their "great walk with God." Jesus is always "Johnny-on-the-spot" with them. He talks to them with such clarity and regularity that you would not be surprised if Jesus asked *their* opinion on how to handle a world crisis.

When I hear that kind of talk, I grow skeptical. You might say I fight cynicism, but I digress. That is my issue, not yours. Perhaps they walk in that state of victory, and I have not reached that level. Yet the bottom line of the disciples' story is their closeness to Jesus. He was with them, only a few feet away in the flesh. They knew more about Him than I know because they had spent so much time with Him. They had front-row tickets to many miracles, but now Jesus' seeming lack of concern—His snoring while the storm was blowing—was distressing them.

Their exclamation was pointed: "Jesus, don't You care?" I have asked that same question. Haven't you? Haven't there been times when you looked up and uttered, "All hell is breaking loose in my life. Where are You, Jesus?" It's okay to admit those seasons of life when you cried out in the darkness, "The storms are howling around me, Jesus. Don't You care?"

Look no further if you want to see a picture of capturing His attention in the middle of chaos. While you are gazing, however, pay close attention to details. All the commotion, all the shouting, even the roaring of the winds, did not affect the sleeping Savior. Tornadoes make noise. Watch any news coverage after one has roared through an area. They always find the most flat-speaking, ill-clad person from the bunch and stick a microphone in their face. The inevitable comment? "Sounded like a train coming out of the holler."

Storms make noise, but all the clamor did not awaken Jesus. Such things do not move Him. He's not stunned by nature; He controls it. Satan does not shake Jesus; He has already conquered him. But when His children cry out sincerely, Jesus will move the heavens and earth to get to us. The message from this story is simple: Cry out. Call out like a dying man. In the midst of your hopelessness, reach out to Him in abandon. When you reach the place where no one else can see, hear, or help you, cry out to God.

Our God is given to the cry of the helpless, even when that cry makes no sense in any language. Note how the Lord was moved in Genesis 21:

> So Abraham rose early in the morning, and took bread and a skin of water; and putting it on her shoulder, he gave it and the boy to Hagar, and sent her away. Then she departed and wandered in the

> Wilderness of Beersheba. And the water in the skin was used up, and she placed the boy under one of the shrubs. Then she went and sat down across from him at a distance of about a bowshot; for she said to herself, "Let me not see the death of the boy." So she sat opposite him, and lifted her voice and wept.
>
> And God heard the voice of the lad. Then the angel of God called to Hagar out of heaven, and said to her, "What ails you, Hagar? Fear not, for God has heard the voice of the lad where he is. Arise, lift up the lad and hold him with your hand, for I will make him a great nation" (vv. 14-18).

The boy Ishmael had been left in the desert to die even though he had done nothing wrong, and he cried out to God. Even his mother had distanced herself from him so she would not have to endure the gut-wrenching cries of her dying son. But God was not so far away that He could not hear.

We are never so far removed that we are out of earshot of God. When other people may not be able to hear us, when we may not even be able to speak or cry out loud, God still hears clearly and precisely. God does not listen only when we cry aloud until our throats are raspy and raw. While there is a time for passionate, bellowing prayer, as the Bible records, that's not the only kind of prayer our God can hear. He can hear our prayer before it is uttered (Isaiah 65:24).

It will not be your situation that catches His attention. It's not the slavery in which you are bound or the pressures on your job that will capture His attention. It's not the weight of guilt you feel over sin nor the pain you have due to sickness or loss that motivates Him to answer. It's your cry for His help that will capture His great heart.

In Exodus 3:7, the Lord said, *"I have surely seen the oppression of My people who are in Egypt, and have heard their cry because of their taskmasters, for I know their sorrows."* God saw what was happening to His enslaved people, but He didn't move until they cried out. We need to learn this lesson well. It's going to be our cry that moves the hand of God.

As a pastor, I kept a banner in my office that read, "My church will never grow while my eyes are dry." I saw it every day. It was a constant reminder that it takes my broken cry for God to move in my life. Our cry can bring revival. Our cry can bring healing. Our cry can bring deliverance. Our cry can bring the salvation of our families. Our cry can bring the healing of our land. May God be bombarded by the cries of His children today, longing for His delivering power to take over our lives once more!

Steady Hands

We can work ourselves into a frenzy about how great God is when no storms are on our horizon but then sink like a stone when the first wave hits us. How will we respond when a storm hits us? Are we going to return to the ruts of normality and be ruled by our passions, fears, anxieties, and human nature? Are we going to resort to the customary, merely human ways of response? Lots of crying? Days of disgruntled fussing? Paralysis by fear? Or will we stand fast in the faith that as long as Jesus is with us, our boat is unsinkable? Are we going to be productive people who give witness to His greatness through the storms, or will we be the kind of soil that only produces for a while, until the cares [storms] of life come, and we shrink back? In the storm, we need a steady hand of trust in Jesus.

If Jesus is on board in your life, one of three things will happen whenever a storm heads your way. *First, there are times He will stop the storm from reaching you.* I like this season of life best, but it is probably the least productive time. It's like the time in Simon Peter's life when Jesus directly intervened for him (Luke 22:31-32). Satan had come for Simon Peter. The enemy wanted him badly, but Jesus stood up for Him and prayed. Jesus prevented the testing for a while.

It's always clear sailing for a season. As much as we dread the storm and the time of sifting, we need it to reveal how weak and dependent we are on the Lord. I am convinced that's why He lets storms come our way. Jesus uses them to make us run to Him for protection and reveal our desperate need for His care.

Second, at times, Jesus will stop the storm in its tracks. That's what He did on the Sea of Galilee. He got up and spoke to the storm, and all was calm. I love those times; who doesn't? It's amazing when healing comes instantly. How incredible is it when He speaks, and circumstances change! We are thrilled when He reveals His will with clarity. Shouts of joy cascade when He opens His mouth, and the mountains melt before Him. These are the miracle stories in which we revel. These are the stories written down and plastered all over the place. Miracles! Signs! Wonders! I love them, and I see far too few to satisfy my curiosity.

The third way Jesus deals with the storms is the most common and the least spectacular. This is also my least favorite way He involves Himself in my life. Yet, in my experience, *the Lord's primary way of dealing with our storms is to keep us through them.* He doesn't stop them all from coming, although I wish He would. He doesn't always crush them while they howl around us, though it makes for a great testimony. Instead, He wraps

His power around us and keeps us from harm until the whole thing blows over.

Look carefully at the example I cited a moment ago—a discussion between Jesus and Simon Peter:

> And the Lord said, "Simon, Simon! Indeed, Satan has asked for you, that he may sift you as wheat. But I have prayed for you, that your faith should not fail; and when you have returned to Me, strengthen your brethren." But he said to Him, "Lord, I am ready to go with You, both to prison and to death." Then He said, "I tell you, Peter, the rooster shall not crow this day before you will deny three times that you know Me" (Luke 22:31-34).

We all know what happened to Simon. His failures are renowned. But anyone who knows the rest of the story knows that through the storm, Jesus' prayer kept him, and he rose to become a shining star in God's show during the pioneering days of the early church. God kept Peter through the hurricane of his testing, failure, and restoration. Because of the Lord's presence, Peter rose from the ashes of defeat and became the glowing firebrand for the Jesus he once denied.

What matters is not *how* Jesus gets you through storms but that He gets you through them. It may be more fun to look out at the dark skies of gloom and see Him shoo them away before they get to you, but that's not always going to happen. Some storms will arise and try to drown you, but the Lord will be with you and see you safely to the other side.

The Needed Anchor

Every boat, regardless of size, needs an anchor. There is a tiny nugget of truth, an anchor for every storm-tossed soul, hidden in Mark 4. It is so sublime that we must not overlook it.

> But He said to them, "Why are you so fearful? How is it that you have no faith?" And they feared exceedingly, and said to one another, "Who can this be, that even the wind and the sea obey Him!" (vv. 40-41).

When the disciples saw the storm, they were so afraid they lost their faith. However, the next few words tell a different story. While they were afraid of the storm, they developed a "mega fear" of the One who calmed the storm. Assuredly, the Jesus we serve is much more to be feared than any storm that may be howling around us. The fear of bankruptcy is great, but the awe of the One who can supply all our needs is greater. The fear of sickness is powerful, but the glory of the One who can heal us is greater. The fear of death has held many people in chains for years, but the grandeur of the One who will raise us from the dead is more stunning. As long as He is with us, we need not be afraid. Let the storm fear His voice. Let the devil fear His glare. Let the circumstance fear His intervention. But let us walk in faith, knowing the power of our God to deliver!

Verse 36 shows us why we must cling to Him as mightily as possible: "*Now when they had left the multitude, they took Him along in the boat as He was. And other little boats were also with Him.*" There were many other "little boats" along for the ride. They were being pummeled by the waves and winds as well. They were not as large and stout as the sinking ship the fearful disciples were riding. If you think it was tough on board with Jesus, imagine trying to cross that stormy wake without Him. Yet, in the middle of the storm, the deliverance of the disciples had a profound effect on the other boats in the area.

We need to arise, cry out, endure the storm, and let Him have His way in our lives because there are "little boats" coming along. They are watching, learning, and leaning on us. That's why it's important for our children to see us worship, hear us pray, and watch us grapple with God. The little boats need the security the larger vessels provide. And when I cannot, in my smallness, touch the Lord for myself, I need some super carrier of God to reach up and take hold of His hand for me. Be sure of His presence; if not for yourself, for me.

SERMON OUTLINE

Introduction: It may seem we are jumping all over the place to make things fit into a single day in the life of Jesus. We probably are since the Gospel writers were not interested in a chronological account, per se, but in giving us the picture of Jesus as Savior and Mighty God. They would take stories of His life and weave them together to suit their primary target groups. That's why this long, grueling day seems to be scattered through the different writers.

What a day it was! Jesus encountered opposition from the Pharisees and dominated a demon. He taught in parables and ministered to a huge crowd of people. At the end of an exhausting day, He told His disciples to take Him across the lake. Little did they know what awaited them. They would encounter a storm at the end of a long day.

1. STORMY FACTS
    a. They Come
    b. They Come to All
    c. They Come to an End
2. SEARCHING FOR HELP
    a. Struggling in Stormy Weather
    b. Shocked in the Moment
    c. Shouting at Heaven
3. STEADY HANDS
    a. Steering Storms Away
    b. Stopping Storms Immediately
    c. Securing Saints in Storms

Conclusion: A storm at the end of the day presents us with a powerful truth—Jesus is more frightening than the storm you now face. His ability to insert Himself into your life, to protect you in the middle of life's greatest tragedy, is so awe-inspiring that you should tremble more at His presence than the storm. Cry out and watch Him display His wonder in your life. Who knows, there may be some "little boats" watching that will benefit from your experience.

STUDY QUESTIONS

1. What has been the worst storm of your life? How did you feel when going through the strongest part of that storm?
2. Do you ever feel as if God has forsaken you, that He does not care about you and your calamity? What was your main focus during that season of life? How did you regain proper focus and cast your care on the Lord?
3. How are you most comfortable in prayer? Do you think God might allow ill winds to blow in your life to stretch you toward Him?
4. What have you learned about God and yourself through the storms you have endured? What have you learned about the storms?
5. The disciples were stunned when Jesus revealed His power over the storm. Have you discovered Him to be greater than anything you face? How does His glory impact your life today?

6. What are some “other little boats” in your life? Are you revealing to others less mature in the faith the power of Jesus that can be discovered through prayer? What can you do to help others discover this place of refuge?

13

MY FAVORITE STORY

Then they sailed to the country of the Gadarenes, which is opposite Galilee. And when He stepped out on the land, there met Him a certain man from the city who had demons for a long time. And he wore no clothes, nor did he live in a house but in the tombs. When he saw Jesus, he cried out, fell down before Him, and with a loud voice said, "What have I to do with You, Jesus, Son of the Most High God? I beg You, do not torment me!" For He had commanded the unclean spirit to come out of the man. For it had often seized him, and he was kept under guard, bound with chains and shackles; and he broke the bonds and was driven by the demon into the wilderness.

Jesus asked him, saying, "What is your name?" And he said, "Legion," because many demons had entered him. And they begged Him that He would not command them to go out into the abyss. Now a herd of many swine was feeding there on the mountain. So they begged Him that He would permit them to enter them. And He permitted them. Then the demons went out of the man and entered the swine, and the herd ran violently down the steep place into the lake and drowned.

> When those who fed them saw what had happened, they fled and told it in the city and in the country. Then they went out to see what had happened, and came to Jesus, and found the man from whom the demons had departed, sitting at the feet of Jesus, clothed and in his right mind. And they were afraid. They also who had seen it told them by what means he who had been demon-possessed was healed. Then the whole multitude of the surrounding region of the Gadarenes asked Him to depart from them, for they were seized with great fear. And He got into the boat and returned.
>
> Now the man from whom the demons had departed begged Him that he might be with Him. But Jesus sent him away, saying, "Return to your own house, and tell what great things God has done for you." And he went his way and proclaimed throughout the whole city what great things Jesus had done for him (Luke 8:26-39).

I love this story. Apart from the beauty of the Christmas narratives, the powerful images of the Passion, and the hope of the Resurrection stories, this is my favorite story from Jesus' life. If I could only have one story from the life of Jesus to preach, one event to recall, one episode to revel in, apart from the aforementioned foundational stories, this one would be my choice.

Here's how this amazing story sets up. After a long and tiring day, Jesus and His disciples set out to cross the Sea of Galilee. During this single day, Jesus confronted the challenge from the Pharisees and warned them of blasphemy against the Holy Spirit. He then cured a man tormented by the devil and challenged the crowds with parables. The close of the day found Him calming a storm that threatened them with death.

They had, in all probability, left the shore on their way to the land of the Gadarenes somewhere between six and seven in the evening. Considering the time spent fighting the storm and the awesome display of His power, it probably took them three to four hours to make the trip. That would put them on the Gentile shore somewhere just before midnight.

Under a starlit sky, with keepers of the swine looking on, Jesus set foot on the banks of that pagan-dominated region, ready to demonstrate His terrible power and tremendous grace. By the time the sun would rise on that new day, some men would be set free, and a region would make a tragic mistake. But most of all, *Satan would know he was in serious trouble!*

A Terrifying Sight

According to the Gospel writers[1], as soon as Jesus stepped on the shore, He was greeted by a horrifying sight. Of course, that is from a purely human standpoint. In truth, the kingdom of Satan was shocked to the core by a horrific invasion. I think the moment Jesus' sandaled foot touched the ground, reverberations were sent throughout the region, and every demon on that side of the lake knew something was up. Power was preceding Him, and they knew what His power could do.

By and large, people are scared of demons, and rightfully so. They are nothing to toy with. I have talked with all kinds of people who have been terrified by movies such as *The Exorcist.* The possibility of demonic possession is frightening.

That's what met Jesus on that shore. It was late at night, and they were enshrouded in darkness. Being tired added to the suspense and drama unfolding before them. Matthew, in his account, tells us two men approached Jesus. Don't let that bother

---

[1] This account is related here as well as in Matthew 8:28-34 and Mark 5:1-17.

you. Since two men would be delivered (and then serve as witnesses), the Jews would be more prone to accept the story.[2] Luke focused on one man who was the spokesman. However, be assured Jesus didn't leave one well and the other tormented. Every demon on that seashore met his match that evening.

This man demonstrated classic symptoms of demonic possession. He dwelled in tombs that had been cut into the cliffs. We would say the man lived in the cemetery, sleeping on the rotting remains of human corpses. In all likelihood, he dined on the flesh of the deceased. His neighbors were rats, flies, and maggots. Separated from his family and friends, he had it about as bad as it can get.

As his condition worsened and he became more violent, the people from the town tried to tie him up with ropes and cords, but he snapped them. They even tried chains and fetters on his feet, but those were equally incapable of restraining him in his madness. They attempted to lock him up as a means of protecting him and the community, but that did no good. He was relegated to living among the rotting remains of humanity.

Hear how he lamented. People could hear him crying out at night. Mark 5:5 says he cried out "night and day." The Greek word for *crying* was used to describe the croaking of a raven—an inarticulate, pitiful-sounding cry. It was the lament of a man who was being tormented and tortured. I think he was trying to say, "Somebody, please help me!" Even if they could have understood him, there wasn't anyone around who could do anything about his situation.

Ah, but Jesus was on His way. He left the religious crowd, walked away from the needy crowd, and stopped a storm sent

---

2 Matthew wrote to an audience who understood the necessity of having at least two witnesses in order for something to be established. See Deuteronomy 19:15.

to destroy Him . . . *all so He could meet this man's demons head-on.* If you feel you are beyond help, "Cry on!" When people around you don't understand what you're saying, "Cry on!" When people around you are frightened by you, "Cry on!" There is One on the way who can do what no other can do.

Look at his lacerations. Again, Mark pointed out how this man would cut himself with stones. Taking sharp rocks, he would shred his flesh in agony. Self-destructive behavior is a hallmark of demonic activity.

Finally, look at his lunacy. He was so overwhelmed and possessed, this man had lost track of where he ended and the demons began. Under the power of the demons, he called himself "Legion," using a number familiar to the disciples. The Roman legions this man had seen in his life consisted of five to six thousand soldiers. This poor guy didn't know who he was or what was happening. He was a lunatic.

Adding these symptoms together, we see his hopelessness. He was dominated by Satan, controlled by forces over which he held no power. He was utterly lost.

Personal Devil?

Let's pause to address some modern thoughts about demons. Three main viewpoints exist about the demonic, or Satanic, in our world.

First, there is the "enlightened" view. Essentially, these people don't believe in the existence of demons or a personal devil. Their diagnosis of this poor guy would be purely psychological. Their method of treatment would include drugs, therapy, perhaps hypnosis, and any other methods that would appear to bring some relief.

I am thankful for the progress made in the field of mental illness. I respect those doctors' education and their dedication to service. But it wouldn't matter how many brilliant PhDs or MDs come together; the moment they deny the existence of demonic forces, I would disagree with them. I am aware that, compared to theirs, my education pales, my vocabulary is elementary, and my sophistication is rudimentary. But my Lord spoke to the demons in this man and set him free. I choose to believe the words and actions of Jesus over the most learned and respected people of the day without reservation or apology.

Satan is real, and demons can possess a person. I think it may be more common than we suppose. Some of the horrible crimes we see go deeper than just a warped human psyche. I am convinced there is a devil who works behind the scenes to kill, steal, and destroy. We are deluded to think the only way Satan operates is in a manner exactly like in the New Testament. He is shrewd, crafty, and utterly deceptive.[3]

The second point of view is the opposite of the first. The "excitable" see a demon behind every bush. They believe demons cause every bad thing. If you have a headache, it's not because you slept poorly, or have stress, or eye strain. No, your headache is caused by a demon squeezing your head like a grape. If you have a fender bender, your carelessness had nothing to do with it; a demon caused your car to smack into that other vehicle. If you get a cold, it wasn't the germs a co-worker spewed when they sneezed; a demon brought it on you. If you lose fifty dollars, a demon lifted it from your possession. This excess is as bad as denying any demonic activity at all. It will drive you crazy! (Oops, they would say a demon will drive you crazy.)

---

[3] When Paul dealt with the Corinthian church, Satan was masquerading as "an angel of light" rather than the prince of darkness (2 Corinthians 11:14).

Third, I offer a middle-of-the-road opinion; I will call it an "everyman's" position. Simply put, demons exist, and they war against us. While they seem to flourish in less civilized, less educated, and poorer places, their influence is readily present in America.

Evil does exist and takes on many forms. However, some things we call "evil" are biological problems that can be corrected with medicines or surgery. Other problems are environmental and can be significantly helped with therapy, counseling, and other mental health procedures. However, some people are simply evil. They are filled with hatred, murder, and avarice, and they can't be made better with medicine or therapy. There is only one hope, and it is called *deliverance*. Thank God we have a Deliverer!

Back to the scene before us. Jesus stepped on shore, and suddenly, there he was—a man full of the devil. A careful reading informs us that Jesus immediately spoke up, calling for the demons to come out. As soon as the Lord came near, He took action to set the man free. It's then we are told the rest of the story.

Triumphant Jesus

I love the story of a newly saved woman from a biker club who was interviewed on Christian television. When the host, in a nice, religious way, called for her to "curse" the devil, she let go with a stream of obscenities aimed at Satan. Gasping, the host responded that the devil deserved all that was said about him. (I want to curse him, and probably not all my curses would be the "sanctified" kind, either!)

I cannot stand Satan. He is a belligerent, overbearing, oppressive, antagonistic, ardent, hot-headed, duplicitous, pugnacious, bellicose, quarrelsome, good-for-nothing, gooey-gum-stuck-on-the-bottom-of-your-shoe piece of work. I hate how he bullies, manipulates, and lies to people. I hate how he struts around with a "What you gonna do about it?" attitude. I hate how he blinds people to keep them from coming to Christ. I hate how he constantly tries to get us to fail and then mocks and heaps guilt on us if we do. I hate how he so persistently fights against us in our weak places, always trying to get us to go back on Christ, to abandon our faith. I hate how Satan . . .

- Orchestrates the destruction of babies in the womb
- Deludes the minds of the young with drugs, alcohol, and other destructive choices
- Drives men to abuse, women to abandon, and children to attack
- Causes wars for nothing and causes reasons for just wars
- Raises dictators who are mad and bloodthirsty while also corrupting leaders in democracies to act similarly.

What I hate most about Satan is that he does all these horrible things, and *there is nothing I can do about it!* He struts, crows, and calls for all comers, and he takes us on, one by one. Over time, each of us is victimized by him. The godliest saint among us knows how it feels to fall prey to him. We can remember the ringing tones, in our spiritual ears, of his hideous laughter and mocking glee as we have fallen to his devices.

You may not wish to admit your inability to handle him, but it remains true. I take comfort in knowing I am not alone in this number. Moses joins me. So do Abraham, Isaac, Jacob, David, Elijah, Elisha, Isaiah, Paul, Peter, James, and John. Every name in the Hebrews 11 "hall of faith" identifies with my sentiment. We all hate him because he is bigger, better, smarter, and more cunning than all of us put together, and there is nothing we can do about it on our own.

I love this story of "Legion" because it shows the real me. I find a companion in the one who is fallen, broken, irreparably shattered. Like this poor man, I am helpless before my enemy.

There is something else we need to understand. Human power always falls short. The people of this town had tried their best—in this case, with steel chains that broke like rotten strings. I hate to, but I must give Satan his due. He is bad. I hate his bragging and his whole demeanor, but he can back his stuff up. I think that's why I love this story so much. There is no mistaking Satan's power.

Here's where the story gets really good. As soon as Jesus hit the shore, He went on the attack. The guy came running at Jesus; why, we do not know. It was dark, and the disciples were still damp from the storm and in awe of Jesus' power in calming the tempest. Suddenly, a lunatic raced toward them. Jesus responded by crying out, "Come out!" At that moment, the war started. Amazingly, at that same moment, the war ended. The forces that drove this poor guy crazy fell in agony before Jesus. The power that men could not restrain suddenly quivered like a kitten before the Master. The foes of humanity that had the region terrified of even passing by suddenly met something more frightening than them. What had reigned supreme immediately bowed like a vanquished foe, begging for mercy. I love this story because it tells me, in no uncertain terms, that *Jesus is Lord!*

The demons said, *"What have I to do with You, Jesus, Son of the Most High God? I implore You by God that You do not torment me"* (Mark 5:7). The demons' statement can be translated as,

"Why are you interfering with me, Jesus?" (NLT). The demon that spoke for the others wanted to know why Jesus was there at that place and time. Why had He come to break up their party with that poor soul?

Think of all the ways those demons had shattered this man's life. They had caused him to eat rotted flesh, but that was about to end. They delighted in making the poor man cut himself up, but that was about over. They jubilantly made the poor guy cry out pitifully, but those sounds had been heard for the last time.

Here's the great news: The party Satan has been having in your life—the cycle of despair, the clocklike destruction, the never-ending sense of dread—is just about over. Jesus will show up and break up the devil's party in your place. I know you have tried with all your might, and others have tried with all their ability. Some have prayed for you. But Jesus wants to show up and release His power. When He comes, what you cannot handle and makes you quiver will suddenly fall to the ground in wretched convulsions before Him.

I realize some people cannot identify with my sentiments. They have never had a struggle they could not master nor fought a sin they could not overcome. Some have never had a child turn rebellious and break their heart. Others have never watched a family member fall off the edge and become unreachable. Others have never faced financial wreckage. We have all heard about people who are so super-spiritual that they have never endured hurt, never been offended, or had so much as a bad dream. If that describes you, go ahead and take a nap and pick up a couple of paragraphs later. But, if you are like the rest of us, this image is wonderful. Jesus did not give the helpless man preventative medicine to keep him from trouble. Instead, he rescued this man from a horrible spot. He released His power to wrench a man from Satan's clutches.

Mistakenly, some people think the church is only here to help good people get better. We exist to take the poor and make them middle class, the middle class into the upper class, and the upper class into the really wealthy. We might think the only reason for the church's existence is to show us how to lead better lives, stay away from drugs, and become better family members. All those are wonderful things, but if Legion had been taught every good manner on earth, the result would have only been a cultured class of demons. We need more than information; we need transformation by the power of God. We need more than to dress up to make us look good; we need to demolish the enemy's spiritual strongholds in our lives. We must shift our focus on what is essential and once more have a place where the needy can meet the Deliverer.

For fear that we get too hung up on appearances, look at what Jesus did and did not do when the man *"ran and worshiped Him"* (Mark 5:6). Jesus didn't tell him to rinse with mouthwash, put on new clothes, get a haircut, and clean up his language. He said, by His actions, "I am going to deal with you right here, right now, just like you are. I will reach into the squalor where you live and rescue you." There is probably more to the fact the demonized man worshiped Jesus than we can unpack here. Suffice it to say if we would worship in a similar manner, we might have less Satan and more Savior in our lives.

Jesus re-enacted something a king of Israel did many years prior. Read the young king's account of his life:

> But David said to Saul, "Your servant used to keep his father's sheep, and when a lion or a bear came and took a lamb out of the flock, I went out after it

> and struck it and delivered the lamb from its mouth; and when it arose against me, I caught it by its beard, and struck and killed it" (1 Samuel 17:34-35).

Pay close attention to what David said. Too many of us have a mental image of David sitting on a high perch, watching over the sheep. Perhaps you see him playing a harp or blowing on a flute, making music to God. Suddenly, he spies a lion creeping along the edge of the woods. Ever watchful, David takes his sling, fires a long-range shot at the beast, and kills him. Later, a bear tries to sneak in and wreak havoc. If that's your idea of what David did, you're not paying close enough attention. A lion and a bear had a lamb in their jaws when David attacked. He wasn't shooting long distance at a possible predator; he engaged in hand-to-hand combat, rescuing a crying lamb clinched in a beast's fangs.

Forget the idea that church is about a preacher telling "here's-how-to-improve-your-life" stories to a bunch of whitewashed saints who are already perfect. The real Gospel is about a Savior who will come right up to the snapping jaws of alcoholism and snatch you out. The real Jesus will walk up to the snarling beast of crack addiction and slap him so hard that he drops your child. This real Jesus will walk up to cancer, stare it in the eyes, and strike it over the head with a rod, causing it to drop you on the spot. Jesus will come to where we are—bound, blind, begging, desperate, unable to help ourselves, addicted, weary—*and strike the very power holding us hostage to set us free.* I love this story because it screams, THERE'S HOPE FOR ME! Satan may have been having his way with me, but when Jesus shows up, He disbands the party of my attackers, and I can go free.

Telling Our Story

On the surface, it is disconcerting when the man is set free. I am not talking about the pigs running off the cliff. All that shows is that pigs are smarter than people. They were not going to let the devil drive them, so they committed "sooey-cide"—sorry, I couldn't help myself.

What's captivating is the interaction between Jesus, the man, and the townspeople. By the time everything settled down, the man was clothed and in his right mind. The keepers of the pigs ran into town and brought the delegation out, no doubt to cover their tracks. The townspeople were seized with fear of Jesus, and they demanded that He leave the area.

I am amazed by their reaction. They never got rid of the demoniac, but the moment he was set free, they became so afraid of the One who delivered him that they asked Jesus to leave. We are a fickle and stubborn bunch, aren't we? We will tolerate all sorts of inconveniences as long as they don't cost us money. Remember, this man was so bad, they couldn't pass that way. They would take a circuitous journey to keep from coming close. Yet the moment it cost them something, suddenly that guy wasn't so bad.

Marvel with me at the grace and mercy of Jesus. The guy sitting at the feet of the Deliverer wanted to go with Him. I can understand that. Who wouldn't have wanted the same? Amazingly, Jesus refused him. That's odd. One would think Jesus would want all the disciples He could muster. Yet here we find Jesus telling this man to go back home. Why would the Master demand such a thing?

Consider what his life was going to be like moving forward. Everyone would talk about him. They would point to his scars. They would tell degrading stories about how he once lived.

Undoubtedly, people would mock him and marvel at the amazing change that had transpired. When asked about his life, his response would be simple. All Jesus asked of him in return for the incredible life change that had taken place was to be a witness to the glory of God: *"Go home to your friends, and tell them what great things the Lord has done for you, and how He has had compassion on you"* (Mark 5:19).

If you are looking for a concise way to tell your story, there it is: Tell about the *great things* God has done and His *compassion on you.* That's your task. Tell people how much God has done for you and how He has had mercy on you.

Every time somebody whispered about how this man used to eat rotting flesh, he could loudly say, "Yes, but let me tell you what Jesus did for me." Every time some insensitive accuser said something about his scars, he could tell his story of being driven by demons until the Lord was merciful to him.

I know this man became a witness because the next time Jesus came to this area, thousands of people came to meet the One who had set that man free. This story of mercy and power had a tremendous effect, and it still does today. My favorite story! May you and I encounter the Lord's incredible power and make His story known to the people around us.

SERMON OUTLINE

Introduction: I love this story. Apart from the Christmas and Easter narratives, this is my favorite story from Jesus' life. It displays the amazing power of Jesus to overrule powers I cannot withstand. It puts the kingdom of Satan on notice that One greater than me is present. It gives me hope that in my broken world, there is One stronger than the strongest assailant I will ever face. Even when Jesus has engaged and conquered every attack launched against Him, He has time to come to me and enact victory in my life.

1. A TERRIFYING SIGHT
    a. Power from Jesus
    b. The Reality of Possession
    c. A Personal Devil
2. TRIUMPHANT JESUS
    a. Cursing Satan
    b. Crushing Satan
    c. Calling the Hopeless
3. TELLING OUR STORY
    a. Savior Smarter than Me
    b. Shameless Greed on Display
    c. Sharing Your Story

Conclusion: This man was successful in sharing his story. The next time Jesus came through this region, He was not met by a couple of madmen. Instead, He was greeted by throngs of people who wanted to meet the One who could set them free. May you and I encounter this same powerful Jesus and make His story known to the people around us.

STUDY QUESTIONS

1. What do you believe about demons? Is your belief based on what is taught in Scripture or the opinions of skeptics? What does the Bible teach about demon spirits? Where do you stand on the three options offered about demonic spirits?
2. Describe the results of the works of Satan you have witnessed. How do these things make you feel?
3. Have you ever encountered a hopeless situation? How does this story reveal the ability of Jesus to help you even when no one else can assist you?
4. What is your story of deliverance? Are there markers in your life you can point to as evidence of God's grace acting on your behalf?
5. How can you better share your story with others so they might want to meet the One who set you free?